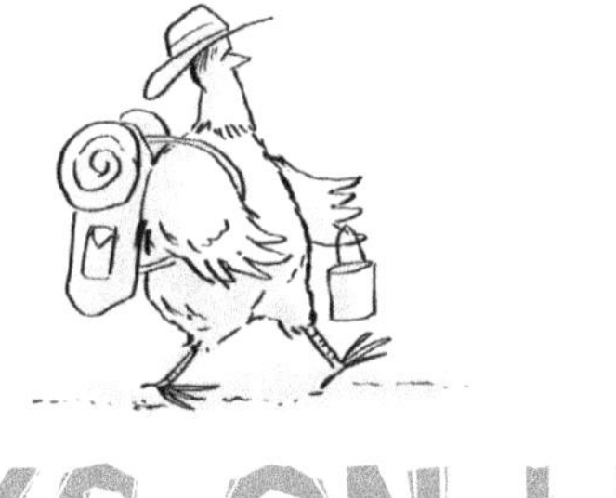

CHOOKS ON LEAVE

The first-ever definitive guide
to Australia's best holiday accommodation
for chickens

Tom Slater

Chooks on Leave

15 Landstrom Quadrant Kilsyth Victoria 3137
Email: tomnjune@bigpond.net.au

ISBN: 9780648981305

Disclaimer: no reliance whatsoever should be placed on any particular claims in this publication. While a good deal of information is factual, it should be obvious that much is pure invention, if not downright incorrect, including the names given to many of the properties listed. No responsibility is taken by the publishers, the author, The Deptartment of Tourism, Havapek Chookfeed, Book-a-Chook or anyone else for that matter for any consequences resulting from reliance on the information provided, whether true or false.

However the names of locations and roads are genuine.

Profits from the sale of this book will be donated to the support of Indigenous ministry.

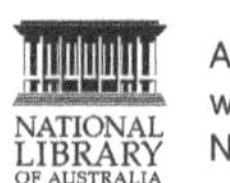

A catalogue record for this work is available from the National Library of Australia

Design and cartoons: Ivan Smith, Communiqué Graphics, Lilydale
Printed by IngramSpark

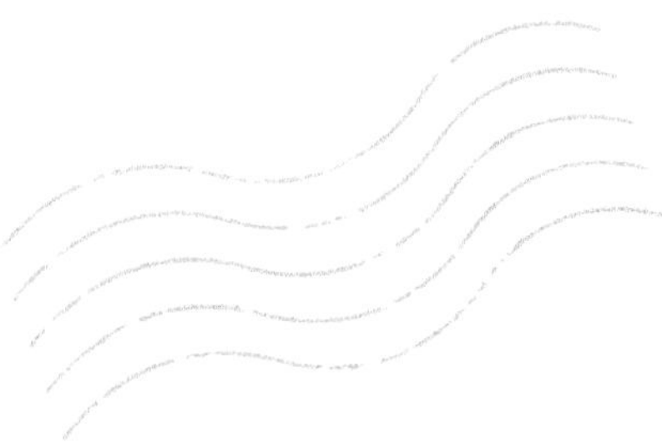

WHAT THEY ARE SAYING ABOUT CHOOKS ON LEAVE

'As a young man I met Tom Slater as he led camps I attended, and found him one of the funniest men I knew. I didn't know he was also a brilliant sketcher. This book is a great match of Australian sketches with wicked humour. A true gem.'

Tim Costello AO
Australian National Living Treasure

'Laughter is one of my favourite pastimes, and it's exactly what the world needs in a time like this. Tom entertains – not only in his exceptional way with words and wit, but with insane talent, using a humble pencil, as he takes the reader on a spectacular tour of Australia in the most unexpected and delightful way. Every chook lover, or person with a sense of humour, will enjoy a light-hearted chuckle in these pages.'

Jodie MacCartney
Community development worker, Klong Toey slum, Bangkok, Thailand

'I have sometimes had to sleep in irregular places. Stranded once in the far north of New Zealand, once or twice under bridges of no particular note, a couple of times in schoolyards, once in a thicket in East Germany. It's never a luxury. In spite of the assertions of many who call themselves my friends, I am not a chook. But if I were, I would be glad of a guide to tell me where to go. Here it is, with pictures. This book is the place to suss the whole thing out. I could roost in a couple of these places myself.'

Ken Edgecombe
Senior teacher, writer, editor and public speaker, New Zealand

'Love the book – fantastic! When I first saw the title, I thought lockdown had finally pushed you over the edge, but now I fully get it, and it's a ripper. Please ship and invoice me a copy when they roll off the press.'

Gary Williams
National Director, Christian Ministry Advancement (CMA)

WHAT THEY ARE SAYING ABOUT CHOOKS ON LEAVE

'I commend this most excellent guide to hen-lovers everywhere – indeed to anyone eager to launch into a virtual Australian adventure in *Chooks on Leave*. With brilliant illustrations clearly described, you will be able to choose and book that tour for your faithful layer. Why not send the whole henhouse?

Staying with us on work trips to Sydney years ago, the author was a magnet for our dog, Inga, who insisted on being remembered to him in all our correspondence thereafter. So this little volume is no surprise, revealing that same intuitive understanding of animals and birds. Read it, savour it, and find what the biblical proverb describes as the 'good medicine of a merry heart'.

Kathi Cohen
co-founder of Moringa Associates, practising peacemaker

At last, a long awaited injection of compassion for those in Pandemic isolation; a fable of ordinariness that touches on deep and profound life concerns. Tom Slater's beautifully observed drawings of fascinating places present an enticing travel brochure for all overworked and deserving chooks. Accurately drawn sheds, public buildings and quiet laneways suggest desirable holiday destinations for chook families; places that are less visited, less 'touristy', less loved and often less known.

So what an enjoyable fable! *Chooks on Leave* enables us to leave the world of logic and convention, for just a little while. It immerses us in the wonders of imagination, yet it also allows us to think outside our own small bubble, to see ourselves in the universe, in the world, in Australia, locked in our own backyard but alive, thriving and just loving drawing our everyday world of very ordinary things. Tom, we love the ordinariness of your drawings; simple sketches, roughly drawn yet with astute understanding of tone, perspective and mood, evoking a homely sense of location.

Lee Emery *(Ph.D.)*
Voluntary Guide NGV and former Associate Professor The University of Melbourne

WHAT THEY MIGHT HAVE SAID IF THEY HAD BEEN ASKED

'At last – we've been waiting for this. For too long the recreational needs of laying hens have been overlooked. Slater's intuitive understanding of chicken psychology and his ability to draw out the features of each holiday resort, (ha ha, draw out, get it?) are evident throughout, albeit on alternate pages. Essential reading for hens, poultry farmers and backyard chook owners alike.'

Feathers magazine

'Cape York welcomes this initiative. Bound to eventually boost chook tourism throughout Cape York.'

Isa Brown,
Mayor of Chooktown

'A timely book for stressful times'

Dr Anna Filactik, *FRACPHP,*
President, Royal Australasian College of Poultry Health Practitioners

'Disappointing. No mention of Surfers Paradise, Longreach, Tweed Heads… oh that's in NSW is it? Anyway, near enough.'

Anaesthesia Pallachook,
Premier of Queensland (by phone)

'Combines scientific insights and everyday practical relevance. This book is a circuit-breaker in the attempt to understand and cater for hen health.'

Heinrich von Chickenburger,
renowned scientist and winner of the Chooker Prize in 2004 for his magisterial volume 'The Mental Health of Hens – The identification of cranial abnormalities in hens of the species Gallus Domesticus, their relation to brain architecture and mental health, and the development of therapeutic strategies for treatment consonant with uninterrupted egg-laying', University of Rhode Island 1997

'Henz everyware will welcome this buk. A brake-threw. Finally a human takes us seeriusly.'

Imelda Henry,
Head of Communications, International Union of Hens, Geneva

'A feast – figuratively speaking of course.'

Chicken Digest

Dedicated to

Aunty Jean Phillips

woman of faith, hope and love

indomitable warrior for her people

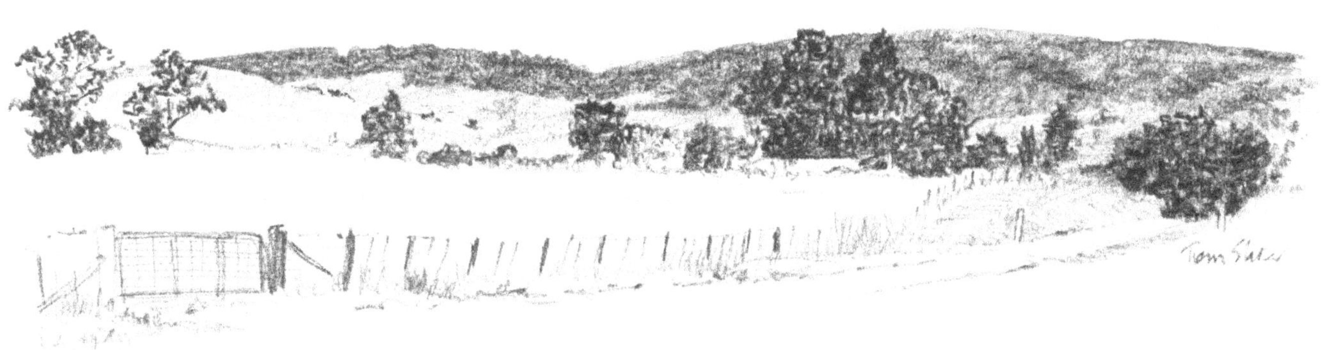

Roadside near Alexandra

PREFACE

Every good hen deserves an annual holiday – a good lay-off as it were. This new and original holiday accommodation guide is endorsed by the Chicken Branch of the Department of Poultry and Environment, and the Department of Tourism. Our government is committed to the welfare of every Australian chook – except for roosters that peck children, and those that crow too early in the morning. A good holiday can bring greater mental health, and new enthusiasm for the all-important task of boosting the national economy by laying eggs.

This publication is directed at laying hens. Roosters, turkeys, geese, ducks and other poultry should consult the Department of Tourism or the Royal Poultry Club of Victoria's Accommodation Guide.

We are indebted to Friends of Poultry, the editors of *Chook Digest Australia*, and the wonderful staff at *Feathers Magazine*, for bringing this invaluable guide to the chook public, and for the generous sponsorship of Havapek Chookfeed and Book-a-Chook. But above all we thank Whiter and Tailplane, two hens without whom this guide would never have seen the light of day, and the author, whose unparalleled understanding of the social and psychological needs of laying hens is evident on every page.

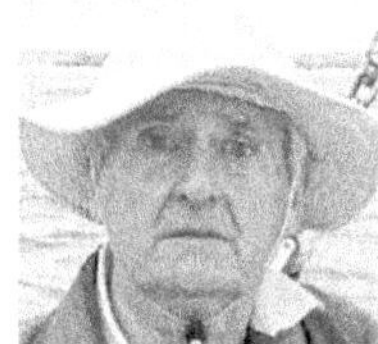

Henry Henderson
Minister for Tourism

AUTHOR'S NOTE

Some explanation seems appropriate, considering the somewhat unusual subject matter of this little book.

Its origin lies in a correspondence between Whiter, one of my own hens, and Kaira, a four year old girl whom Whiter and I (at the age of 75) had fallen in love with. I wrote down the letters, as dictated to me each week by Whiter, but I wanted to include some picture or other with each letter. It occurred to me that I could simply enclose one of my own sketches. And what more appropriate subjects could there be than the numerous old sheds and other nesting places which I had recorded in the course of our travels in Australia. This, to cut a long story short, is how it all started.

The text is generally addressed both directly to the literate chicken, as an indication of respect for her intelligence and reading ability, and to conscientious chicken owners who, in the end, will be paying for these holidays.

The thoughtful person might also wonder how a supposedly serious Christian could spend time messing about with such a project when he might be out and about doing somebody some good. Especially so at a time when millions around the world face horrors every day. The catastrophic COVID-19 pandemic is just one such. Millions of desperate people are homeless, adrift or holed up in refugee camps for years without hope. Countless others lack the basics of clean water, shelter and food, in a world that lacks none of these things, while dictators, elected and unelected, wage brutal wars on their own people to entrench their power and privilege by any means.

I can only plead that in the context of weeks of the COVID-19 lockdown in Melbourne, this was something that I could do, for two reasons at least.

First, I have been given certain modest abilities with words and pencils, and a sense of fun inherited or learned from my parents and other 'elders', all of which should be put to use for the benefit of others – plus the audacity to think people might be interested in it.

Second, humour helps us maintain a balanced perspective, and laughter can be therapeutic. Indeed, according to Australian theologian Brian Edgar, laughter 'has a central role in Christian spirituality'. I reckon he's onto something, because most of the Christians I know best and admire most laugh a lot, and I love that. Edgar quotes GK Chesterton:

> *Life is serious all the time, but living cannot be. You may have all the solemnity you wish in your neckties, but in anything important (such as sex, death and religion), you must have mirth or you will have madness.*

We might add global pandemics, widespread political instability, a frightening loss of social cohesion, escalating mental illness, the absence of hope, and much more. I fondly hope that my little bit of mirth, and a little bit of art, might offset a little of the madness, and gives someone a lift.

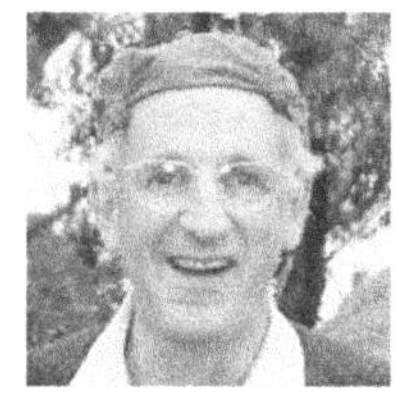

Tom Slater
Kilsyth, Australia, September 2020

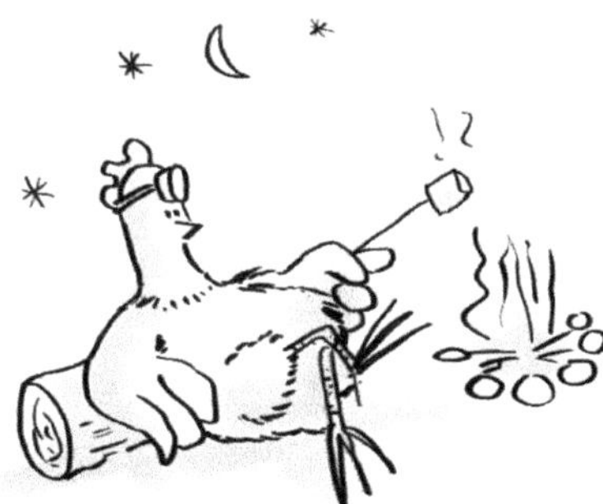

FOREWORD

(*A few odd spellings and phrases below were suggested to me by some literate chooks to whom I showed the manuscript.*) BKJ

This book is a 'must read' for everyone who ever ate an egg, or indeed a chicken.

Tom Slater, (also known by the anagramatic *Late Storm* in literary and meteorological circles as well as Hen Parties) is widely known for his seminal book on organised camping *The Temporary Community* (1984). He is clearly uniquely well-positioned therefore to turn his attention to what may be called organised camping for chooks. Indeed he has poured a lifetime of research and 'paying attention' into this work, in just a few months. It is a useful handbook on the pedantic rules of grammar, a chicken encyclopaedia of random facts, and above all, a definitive answer to the age-old riddle: Why did the chicken cross the road? Obviously it was to take a vacation.

The 'resorts' featured in the book are truly specktacular, with layer upon layer of historic reference and salute to the pioneers of developed rural Australia.

This is a book that you can start anywhere you like – somewhat like a chicken grazing – and find yourself drawn to turn to the next page, and then the next and so on until you find yourself going back to the start to look again. In fact I suggest you STOP reading this foreword now and get on with looking at the pictures and reading every fowl word.

There are some deficiencies in the work which might (or may) alarm some readers – I, myself, was mystified to find no reference to either Attila the Hen or her more recent counterpart Margaret tHatcher, both of whom have materially changed the lives of both people and chooks in significant parts of the world.

It is comforting to note that, as stated elsewhere in the volume, no chook has been harmed in the writing of this book: I can therefore confidently affirm that no chook or human will be harmed by reading it. (Why didn't you stop reading this foreword as instructed above?)

Finally, this is not a book to be read and shelved. It is more a book to *lay down* and *leave lying* about in the house or coop, so that any resident or visitor can peck it up, open it at random and get a little chuckle or even a hearty cackle.

BK Johnson
Melbourne
September 2020

Bruce Johnson is a retired educator with a PhD and extensive experience as an educator and management consultant in Canada and Australia. He also has a rare ability to communicate with (literate) chooks.

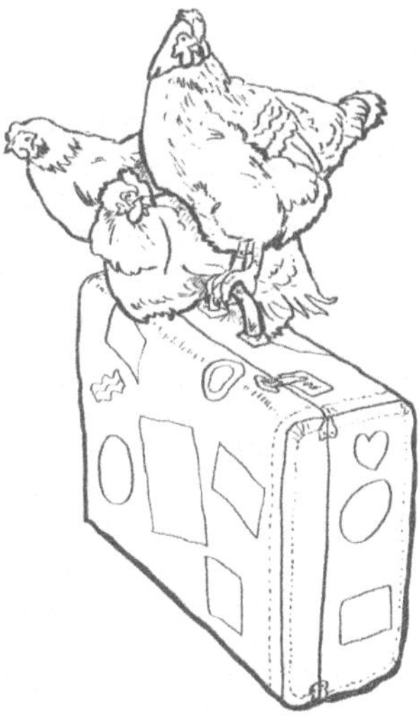

CONTENTS

CONTENTS

INTRODUCTION

The health issues of laying hens, how chooks have led the way in addressing them, and why we have only just noticed

According to Wikipedia there were 23.7 billion chickens in the world as of 2018. I think you will agree that's a lot of chickens. But how many of those chickens have a good holiday even once in their lives?

Even accounting for the short life of chickens bred 'for the table' (thank goodness for euphemisms) and the charmed lives of those lucky enough to be the pets of genuine chicken-lovers, there are literally billions of chooks (and we use the terms chickens and chooks interchangeably) that work away at egg-laying for years, but for whom a holiday can only ever be a dream. Thankfully, however, in Australia at least, an increasing number of caring but hard-nosed (forgive the anthropomorphism) and entrepreneurial chickens have seen the business opportunity that this situation has created, and have been hard at work transforming otherwise useless buildings and even boats, vehicles, old water tanks and other items all over the country into first-class holiday accommodation for chooks.

Most tourists entirely miss these places, since they are invariably either in the backyards of premises, or cleverly concealed behind the facades of otherwise ordinary looking buildings. At the same time transport operators have been slow to adapt to the needs of the increasing numbers of chickens now travelling on a regular basis, so that even where public transport is available to these locations, it is not always practical, *or even permissible*, for chooks to use it. It can be expected that chooks will soon take things into their own hands (yes I know, another anthropo-thingo). Apparently Uberchook is already in the pipeline.

In case it should be thought that some of the enterprises described and illustrated in this small volume seem to be beyond the abilities of the average chook, two things need to be said.

The first is that one should not think for a moment that the entrepreneurial chickens that have led the extraordinary boom in chook tourism are 'the average chook'. Anything but. In the human world, most representatives of the race are not rocket scientists or brain surgeons, but ordinary average people like you and me. Well you anyway. But some have particular gifts of brain or brawn which equip them for particular vocational specialisations.

So it is with chooks. The burgeoning chook tourism industry is a good example. A few gifted fowls have led the way, while the enterprises offering holiday accommodation are run largely by grass-roots chooks of only average intelligence, and well run they are.

Again, it might be supposed that certain *breeds* of chicken are more intelligent, or more enterprising, or just more *lucky* than others. But again the genus Gallus Domesticus is as diverse as Homo Sapiens. Take some examples. Some Australians are good at chess and others at school-crossing duty; or to take a different tack, some Indians like curry while Swedes prefer turnips – to mix up the analogies a fair bit. Similarly some (not many) Rhode Island Reds are good at thinking ahead, and others are not. Many Australorps (but not all) can count up to ten, while some Brahmans have been known to count to fifty or more. Very few of *any* breed can speak English, let alone read or write. It should not be thought that breeds that regard themselves as superior, such as Orpingtons and Plymouth Rocks, are one whit superior to your average backyard Leghorn or Isa Brown. They are just different.

Now the second thing. It is not widely known that recently an increasing number of palaeontologists, biologists and ornithologists, as well as some astute back-yard chook owners, have begun to question the accepted wisdom that human beings are descended (though not directly of course) from chooks. Rather it may be the other way around. Why is this?

Surprisingly, brain size is not the main issue. To be sure, chickens have very small heads, and indeed very small brains as well. But the factor that has led to an evolutionary re-think is behavioural characteristics. For example my chooks peck at the tin can with which I feed out their grain, rather than wait a couple of milliseconds for me to pour it into the feeder.

>>>

Or, when several leaves of silver beet are thrown into the pen for two chooks, both compete feverishly for the same piece – not just sometimes, but *every* time.

For centuries we humans have tended to view such behaviour with a rather superior attitude, despite the fact that we ourselves regularly exhibit exactly the same characteristics. (I mean of course *general* characteristics like greed and stupidity. I haven't heard of any humans who try to eat the tin that their baked beans come in. But who knows?) And so we are surprised to discover what chooks are capable of.

Be that as it may, a vast amount of evidence has been accumulated during the global COVID-19 pandemic to suggest that many humans are far less intelligent than chooks. We need only cite the number of people who claim that having to wear a mask to reduce the risks of COVID-19 is a breach of their human rights.

All of which is to say that we shouldn't be surprised if certain chooks display a remarkable ability to establish new holiday venues specifically designed for their own kind. So with all that in mind, welcome to the journey as we explore in word and pictures the wonderful world of chook holiday accommodation in Australia today.

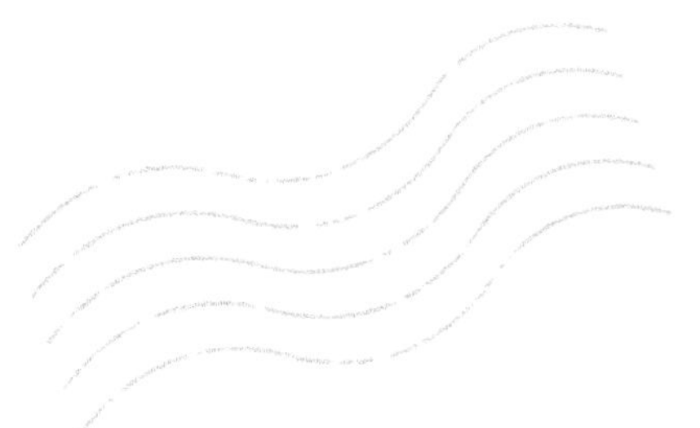

PART ONE

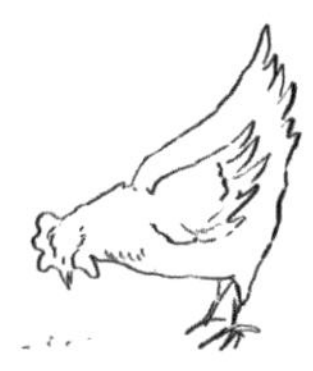

Accommodation for individuals, families and small groups

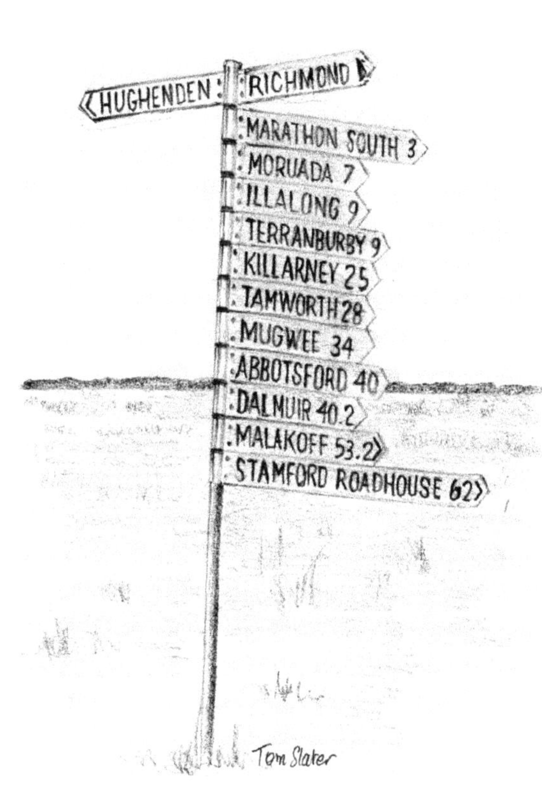

Manna Hill Railway Station, SA

For train buffs, this is accommodation to die for. The old Manna Hill station is on the Indian Pacific railway line. Travel by car or catch the train to Broken Hill and wing a ride with a passing truckie. Thrill to the sound of the train rushing through in the night, but keep your wings tucked in tight or risk being blown to Peterborough down the line.

Food scraps are plentiful at the Manna Hill store a few flaps away on the main highway, but watch for fast interstate traffic as you cross the road. Few chooks have survived a head-on with a speeding 40-tonne B-double.

Manna Hill's official population at the time of writing was 6, except for Anzac Day, when the surrounding people come in. So a quiet time is assured, but your visit will be an encouragement to the locals.

If travelling on to Peterborough, consider side trips to Tattawappa Hill, Winnieminnie, Upper Nackara, Lower Nackara or Nantabibbie.

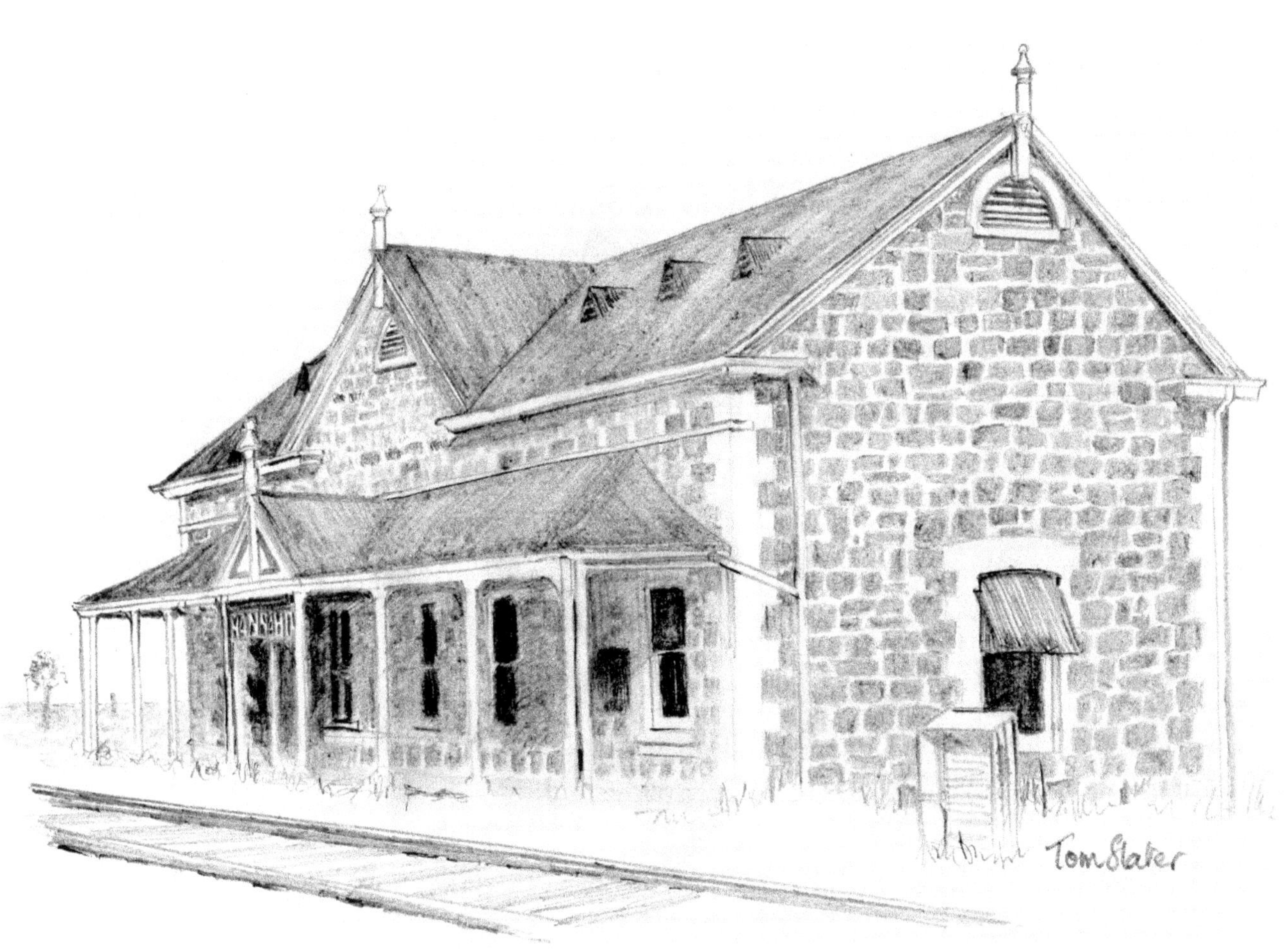
Tom Slater

The Bank, Quorn, SA

Behind the old Savings Bank of South Australia is a hidden treasure. Known these days as The Bank, it is the former chookhouse of the last bank manager. As such it boasts everything a good holiday house could have to offer – purpose-built perches, nesting boxes (handy if you come into lay while away), self-feeders, a dripping tap giving constant fresh water, draft management, security – we could go on. Quorn is a chook's town, with wonderful streetscapes waiting to be explored.

Quorn loses nothing by comparison with other Australian towns starting with Q. It has better weather for chooks than Queenscliff (Vic), more trees than Queenstown (Tas), is easier to pronounce than Quorrobolong (NSW), is easier to get to from Adelaide than Quellington (WA) and is way quieter than Quaker's Hill, a suburb of Sydney, which all explains why it is the preferred destination for the annual Quambatook Chook Safari.

Further afield the Flinders Ranges await the curious travelling hen. Cadge a ride with the postman and spend a night or two at Wilpena Pound.

Famous artist Hans Heysen painted the rugged hills of the Flinders. He also painted *Farmyard scene with haystack and chickens* in 1912 and *Feeding the Chickens*, Hahndorf. Time has not permitted me to complete my research as to other paintings which might include chickens in walk-on roles rather than as central characters.

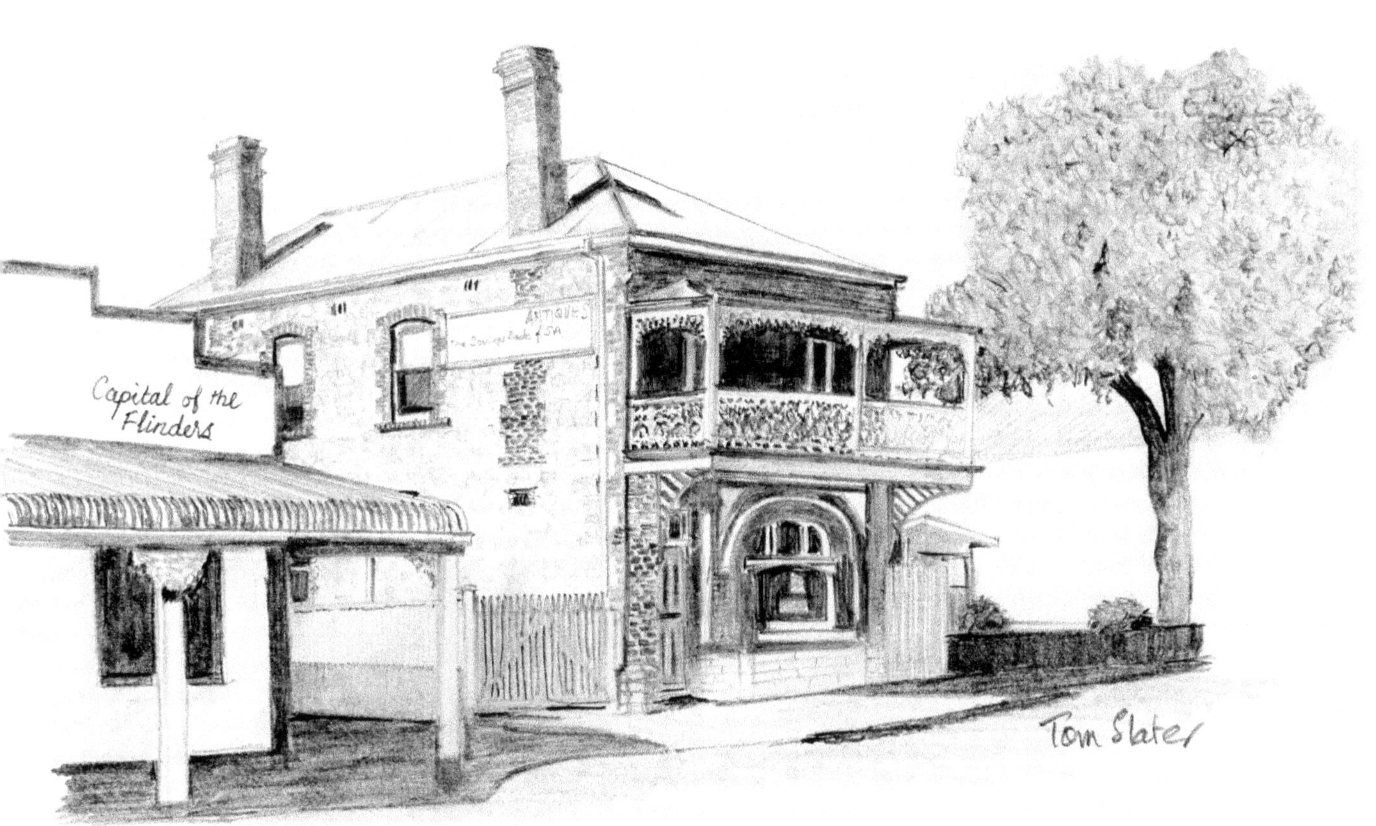
Capital of the Flinders
ANTIQUES
The Savings Bank of SA
Tom Slater

The Bore Shed, Charleville, Qld

Taking its name from the nearby artesian bore, this shed has been classified by the National Trust (Poultry Division), 'in recognition of its superior qualities as a health resort'. Needless to say, there is an abundance of running water rich in minerals, and the shed itself offers a variety of comforts and styles according to your budget.

Visit the Bilby Centre in Charleville before an evening of star-gazing at the local observatory. (It is suggested that visiting chooks practice shutting one eye before the observatory visit, as many chooks find this difficult at first.)

Of course this artesian water originates as run-off from The Great Divide, hundreds of kilometres to the east. This was proved over a period of 90 years by hydrologists from the University of Queensland. A 44-gallon drum of red ink containing a rare chemical marker was poured into a storm water drain west of Townsville in 1897, and in 1987 detectable quantities of this liquid flowed from the bore at Charleville, as had been confidently predicted. Amazing.

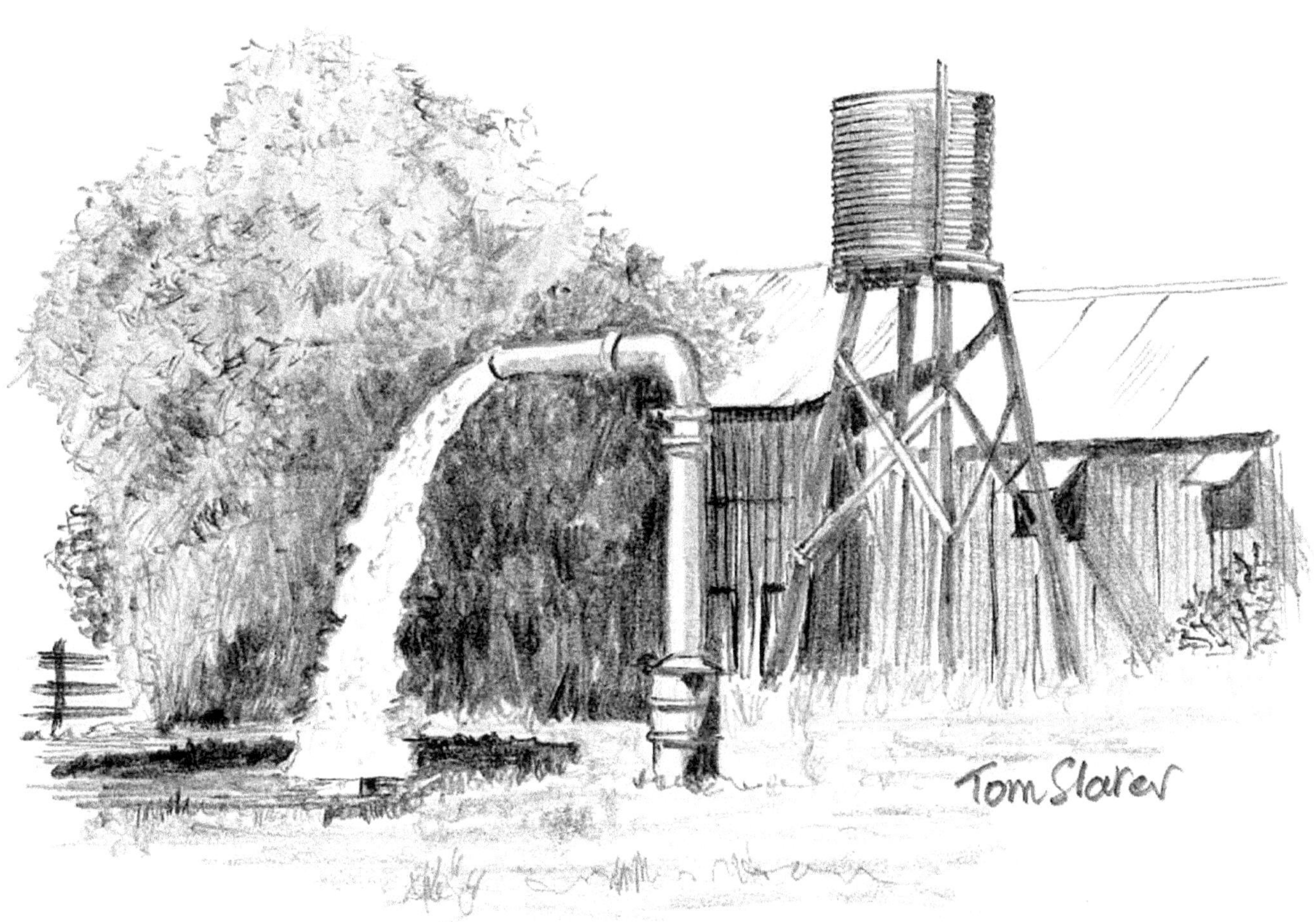
Tom Slarer

Dookie Agricultural College, Vic

This is the holiday place for the serious chook who likes to make use of the holiday break for study purposes. The central buildings of the college illustrated here house the booking office and a library where guests perch comfortably while they study practical subjects such as modern laying arrangements, fodder and chook housing, as well as more technical subjects such as genetics, production values, and even chicken psychology.

The many outbuildings are of great architectural interest, as well as offering a variety of accommodation. For those on a tighter budget, the many bushes and garden plantings offer adequate short-term accommodation in good weather, but avoid term times if possible, unless choosing outbuildings. As a dual purpose facility for humans as well as animals, droppings are not permitted on roads and footpaths.

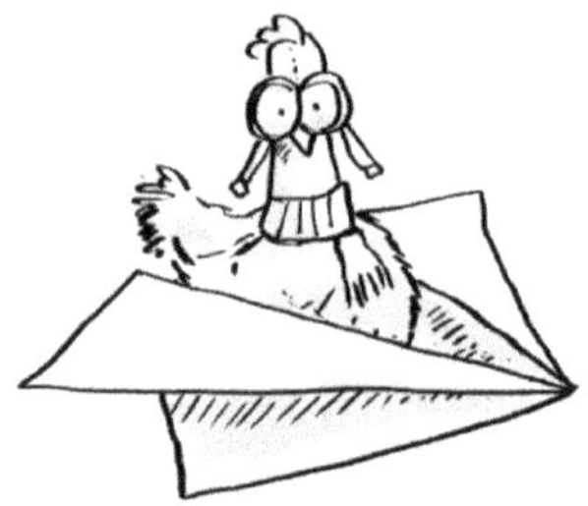

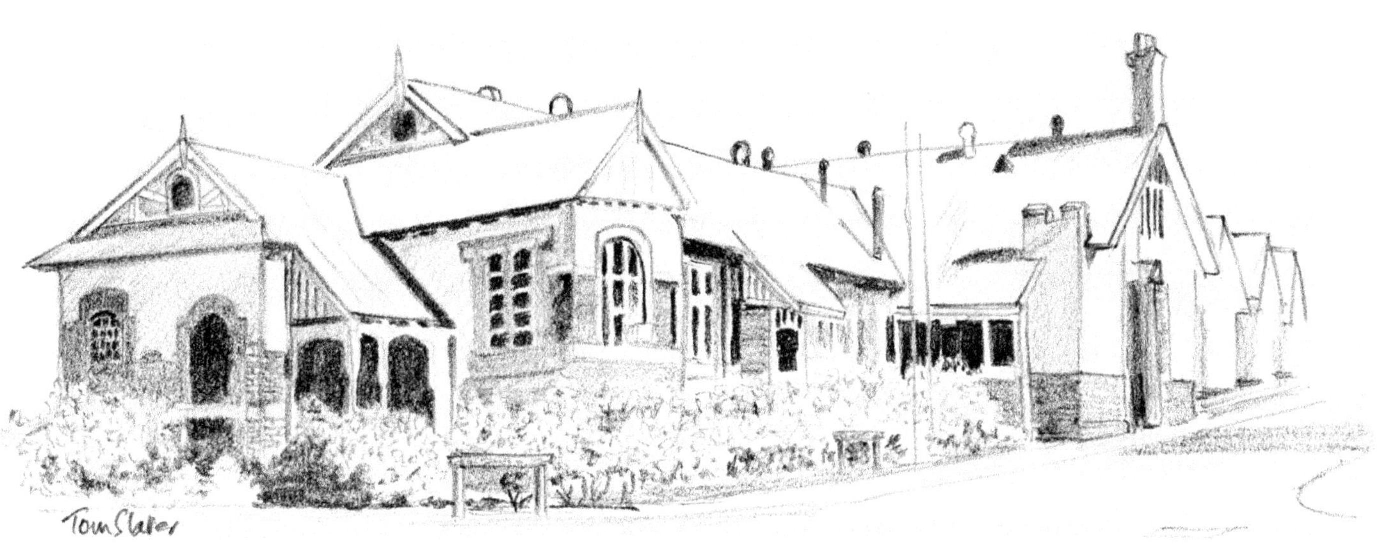
Tom Slater

Dookie College Farm, Vic.

The Dookie farm is exceptionally tidy and well-kept, but there are still a few suitably earthy options for the hen willing to put up with a little extra hygiene. Bookings are made through the college office. No farm accommodation is available at shearing time. Silo-door tastings each afternoon provide an opportunity to try some local grains, but don't try tasting the silo door. Guided tours of the property and livestock can be arranged, and there is a day-care centre for young chickens at a reasonable cost, provided they are toilet-trained. All these activities occur in the farm management area illustrated.

A favourite off-campus activity is a picnic to the nearby Broken River, where honey-eaters and other native birds provide free entertainment for groups if booked in advance.

Dookie, incidentally, got its name from Billy 'Mollydooker' Bailey, an early settler and local boxing champion. Being left-handed, he was nicknamed 'The Mollydooker'. His property was known as 'Mollydook's place', and this was eventually shortened in the characteristically Australian way to 'Dookie'.

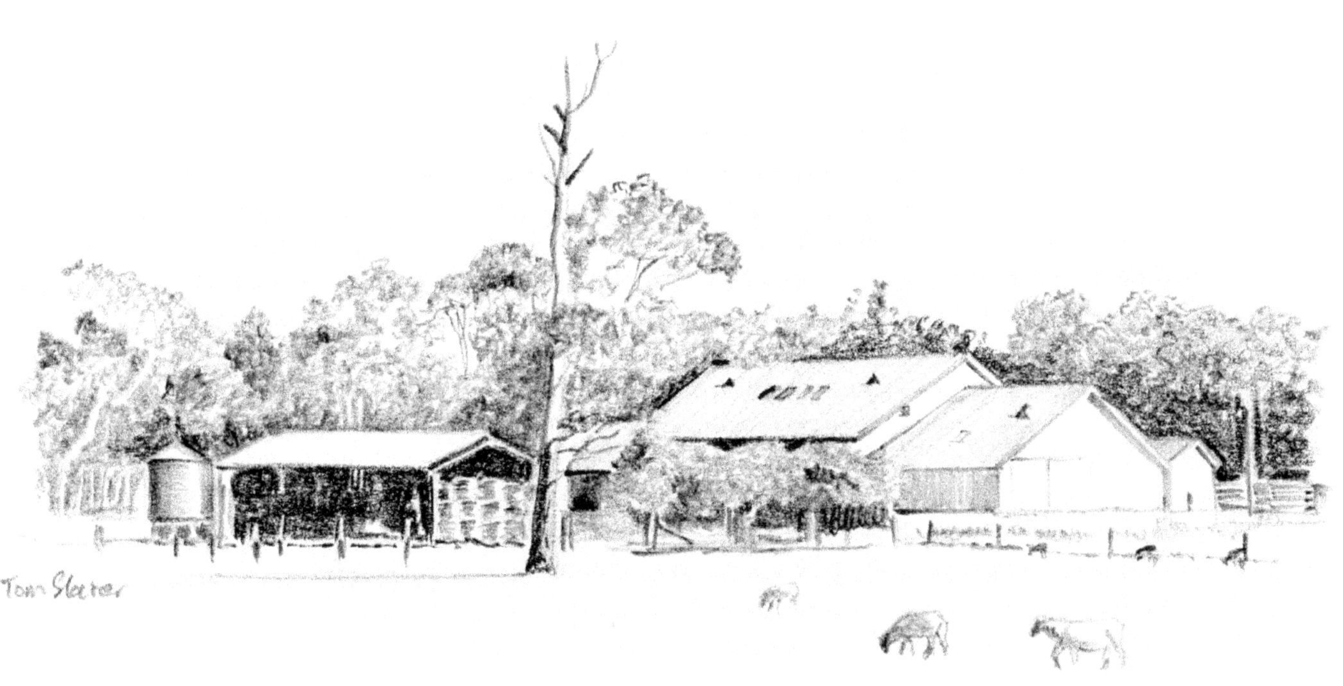
Tom Sleeter

Selector's Hut, Savernake, NSW

This historic building stands on Savernake Station, a heritage-listed working property. The hut dates back to 1876, and became a boundary rider's hut in the 1890s. The cottage itself is too clean for comfort, but the lean-tos at the back and sides offer a more rustic location for a good chook holiday. Savernake is a good stop-off point for chooks travelling from Victoria to Sydney for the Royal Easter Show. The famous Henrietta Johnson detoured here on her way from Tangambalanga to Sydney in 1948, when she won both Champion Layer and Champion Cackler. She attributed her win to the serenity of that first night on the road at Savernake.

A stone monument marking the achievement can be found at the back of this hut, between the grease trap and the rusty downpipe.

Seriously, Savernake Station was designated as a World Heritage site on 15 March 2013, and does in fact have some lovely old holiday accommodation for humans.

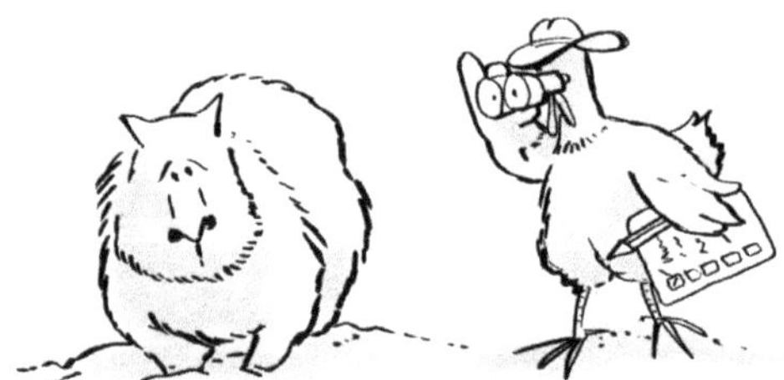

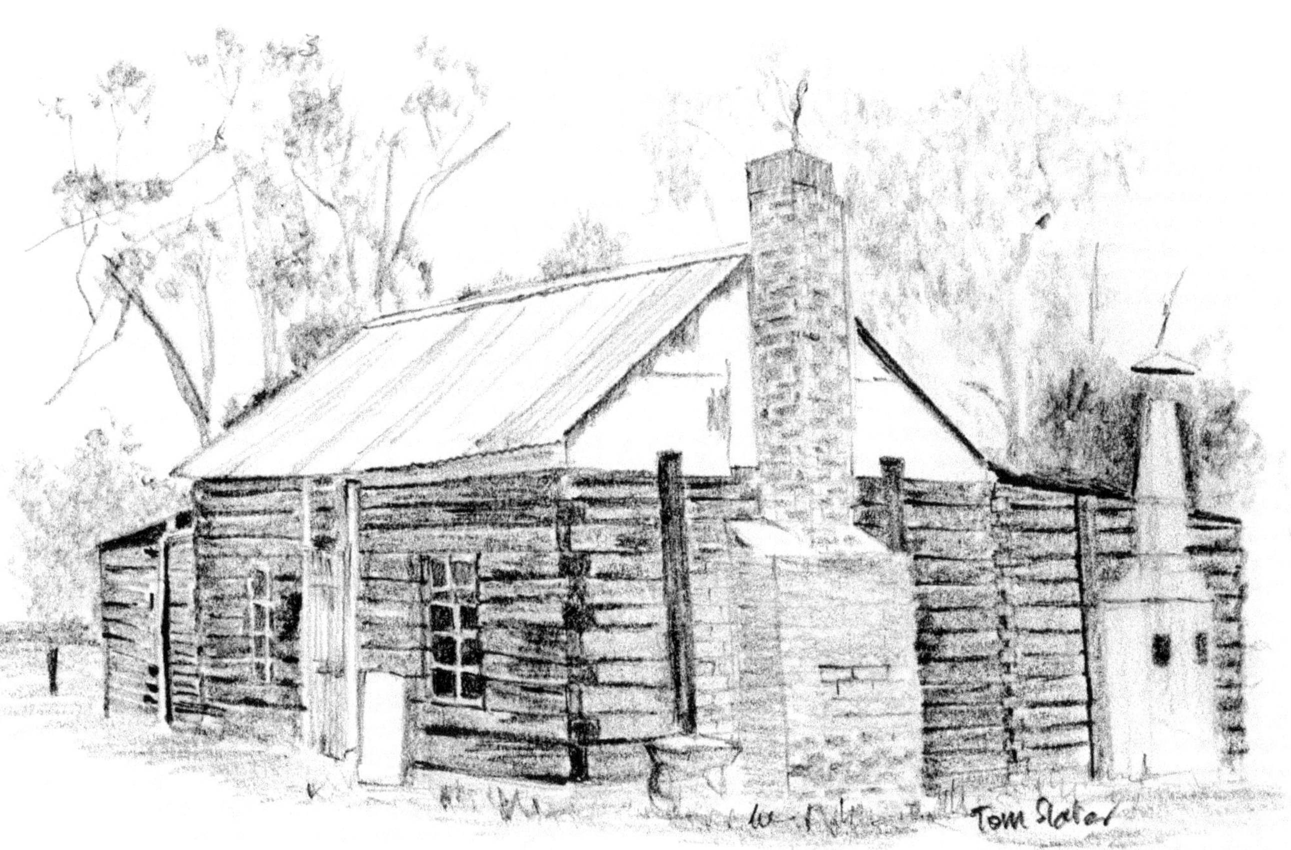
Tom Slater

Grand Astoria, Busselton, WA

Well, *near* Busselton anyway. West of Busselton, on Geographe Bay, next stop South Africa. This exclusive chookotel has direct frontage to the water, and a variety of boating gear and water wings are supplied free of charge to guests. But wait until you see the luxury accommodation, situated beneath the floorboards of the old cottage. Guests are waited on by trained rabbits and the odd wombat. Everything is done for you. If you are not boating you can just sit, lie or perch wherever you choose, and catch up on the latest *Feathers Magazine* or Produce Catalogue. Or be pampered and have a beak and claws trim in the fibro-cement laundry out the back.

Trips can be arranged to Margaret River (wine-tasting, or very rarely for chooks, surfing) and to the Cape Naturaliste Lighthouse. Please note that while Busselton is on the coast, it is nowhere near Broome.

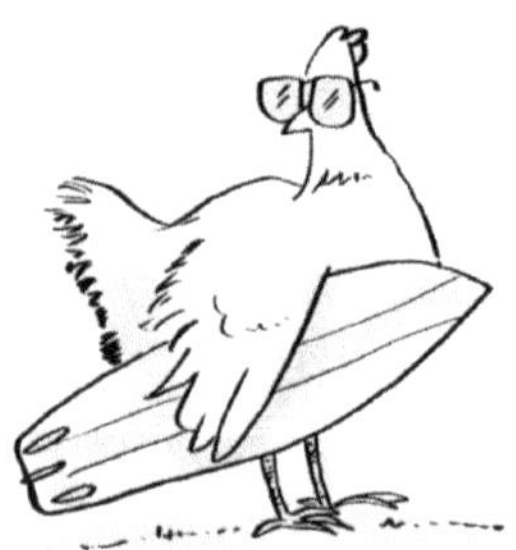

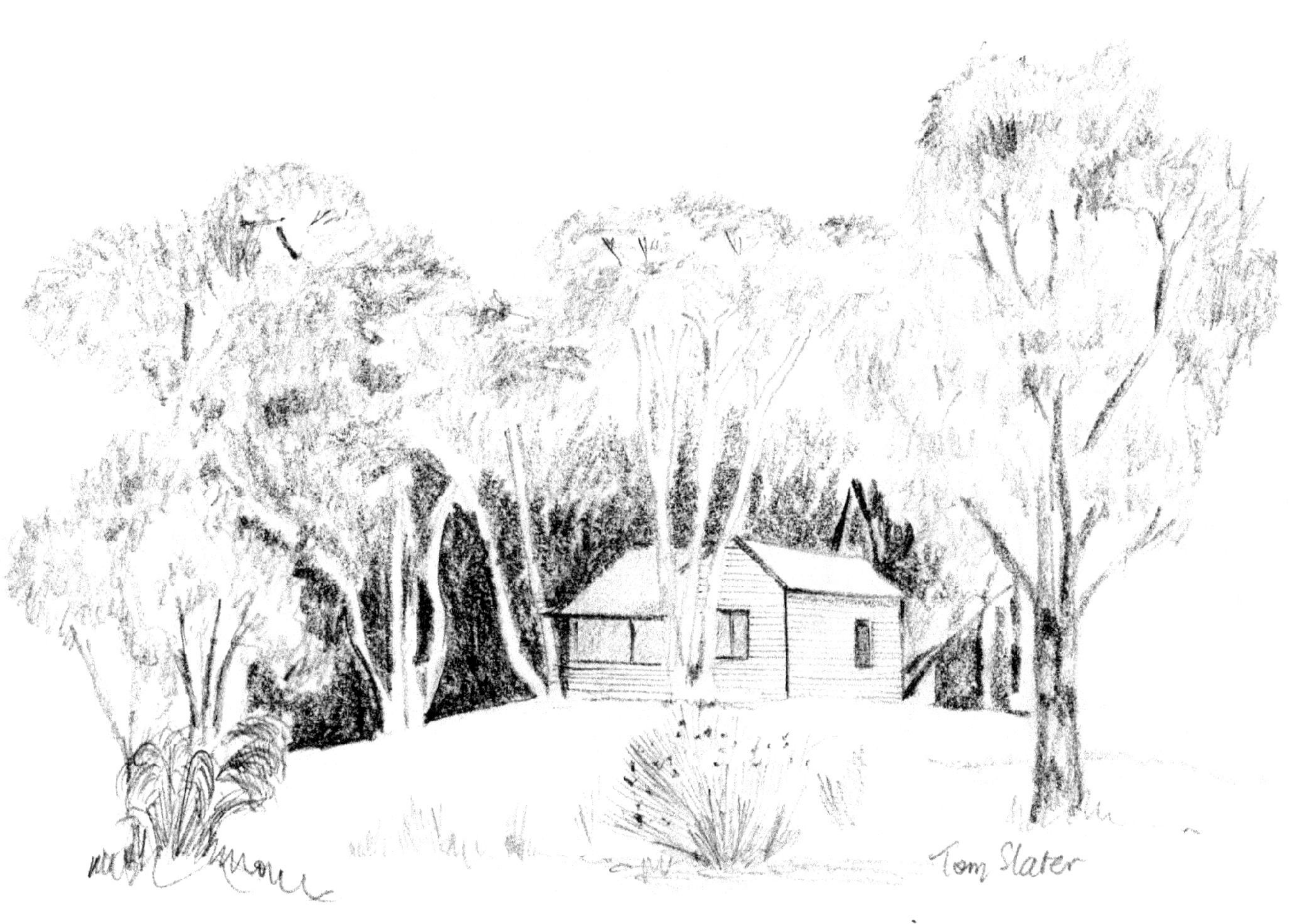
Tom Slater

The Mews, Richmond, Tas

While views of Richmond Bridge and St John's Church are famous, The Mews is a hidden delight. Staying at The Mews offers the best of both worlds – town facilities and rural surroundings. The house yard provides complete security, with the exception of nesting magpies in the spring.

This charming building is solid and well-ventilated, consistent with the beauty and historic charm of the town. Chickens with convict ancestors will find plenty to engage their interest in town, especially the Old Richmond Gaol. Richmond is handy to Hobart airport for interstate chooks, but make sure that you are not going to be moulting during your stay, if booking in winter, as temperatures in southern Tasmania tend to be on the low side, even for fully feathered chooks.

Good scratching areas include the vicinity of the cleverly named 'Cottage on Gunning' on Gunning Street, under the historic bridge (Richmond Bridge is the oldest bridge in Australia), St Luke's Anglican Cemetery and around the tennis club.

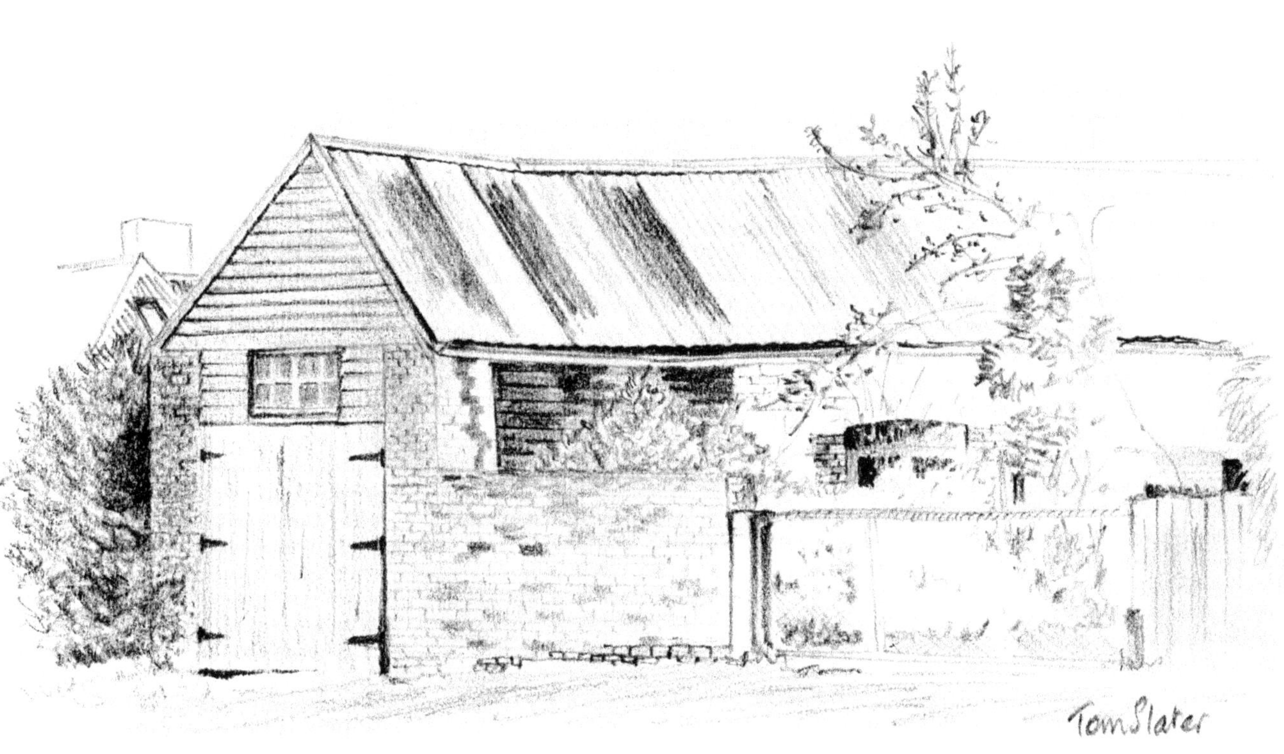
Tom Slater

Bournda National Park, NSW

One of many lovely national parks along the NSW coast with very cheap rates, and one of the most problematic to pronounce. At present you need to bring your own camping gear, sleep in the trees, or work on a night by night basis depending on what caravans are available to camp under. However advance bookings are being taken now for new chookotel units to be opened 'in the New Year'. Check *which* New Year when booking.

Plenty of bushwalking available, but chooks are asked to keep off the tracks. While it is a rare chook that wants to paddle in the nearby ocean, beachcombing is a popular activity. Cuttlefish and shells may be collected in limited quantities, provided they are strictly to aid digestion and beak-sharpening and not for sale to other chooks. Strict penalties apply for non-compliance.

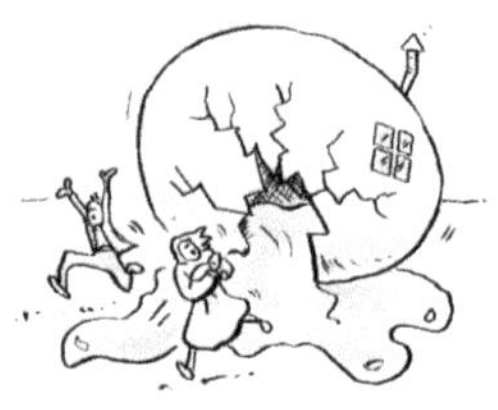

A pallet of 500 bricks weighs approx. 1.5 tonnes. Even assuming very large eggs, it would take at least 15,000 chickens to lay the equivalent weight on any one day, which could explain why we don't make houses out of eggs.

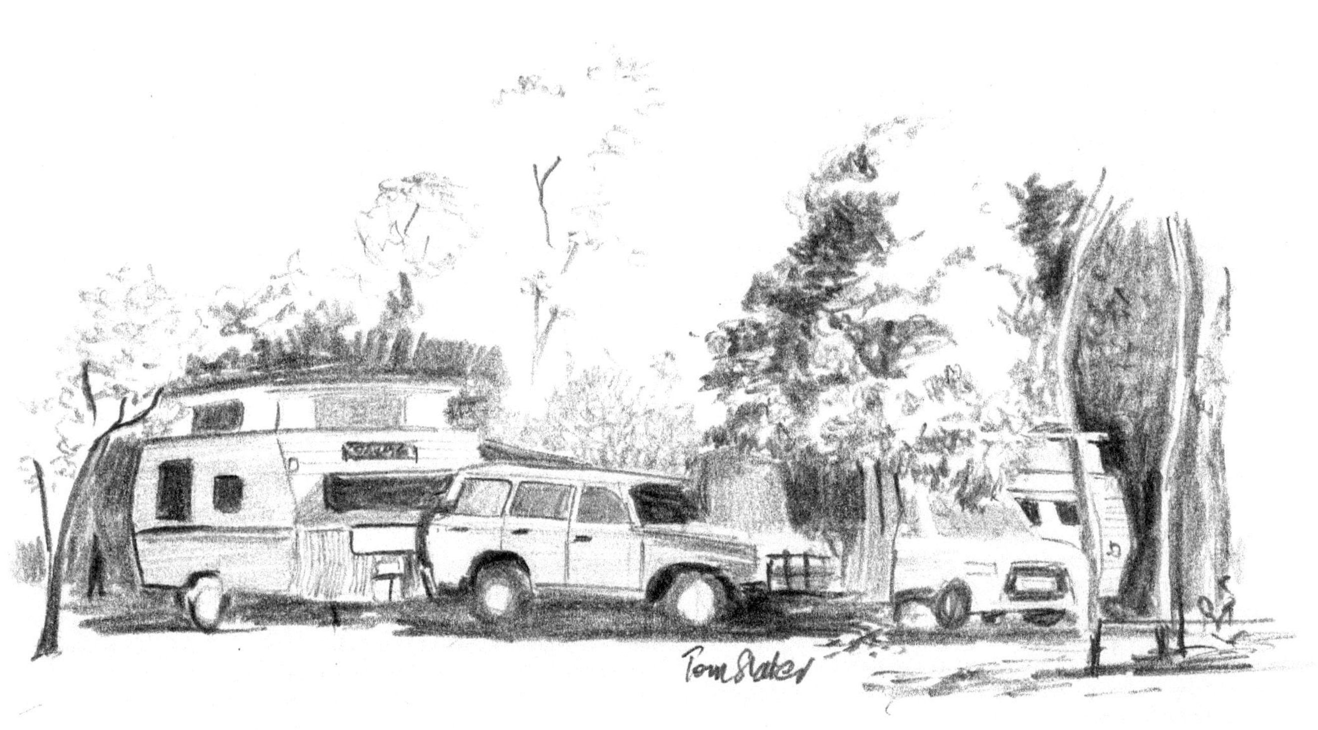
Tom Slater

A-model Ford Chotel, Nhill, Vic

This old A-model Ford, long ago converted into a useful farm ute, has unique characteristics as a chook accommodation unit. In particular, as it is still in good working order, it is liable to become mobile during your stay. The rear tray accommodation is not interrupted at such times, but the inside floor of the vehicle becomes uncomfortably crowded when the vehicle is driven. For the hen looking for excitement, this is the place to find it. A beak-chattering ride spotlighting on a winter's night is the chook equivalent of an Antarctic blizzard. Sleep is impossible, so settle for a quiet rest back in the shed if you prefer a quiet time until the vehicle returns and you can once again settle down for the night.

Lettuce is a particular delicacy served at this farm. Few people know that it was right here that the game of Scrabble was invented. It takes its name from chooks scrabbling around in the ute for their lettuce during and after these wild rides.

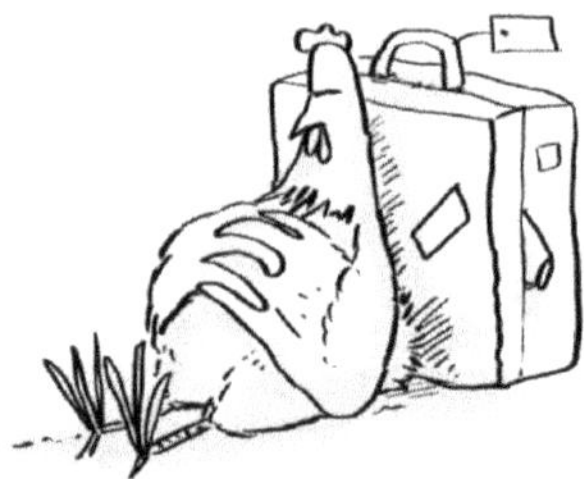

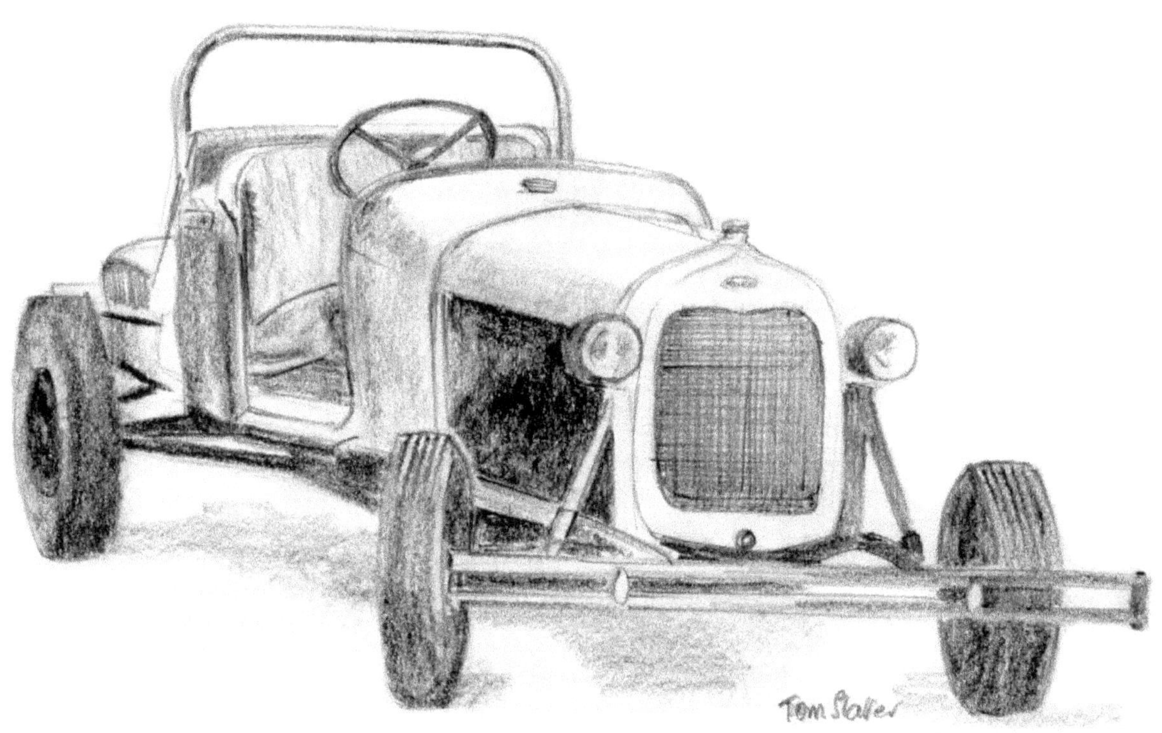
Tom Slater

The Privy, NSW (or Vic)

Looking for a quiet holiday where you won't be interrupted? The Privy sits high on the bank of the Murray River near Echuca. Because of the twists and turns of the river it is hard to be sure whether it is in NSW or Victoria. Set out from Moama or Echuca and follow the river bank upstream until you see it. If you are on the wrong side, simply construct a raft and paddle across.

Boasting wonderful views of the river through missing boards, The Old Privy provides comfort at an affordable price. Wake up to the faint smell linking you to the days of human occupation. Nearby vineyards provide delicacies at the right time of year, while keeping an eye out for the whistling kites which circle overhead around the nearby abattoirs. Easy access, and no keys required. Although House Boat Hire businesses still refuse to hire their boats to chickens, many hirers will give chooks a ride into Echuca for shopping or sightseeing. Just flap a wing as they approach and see what happens.

Footnote: The Old Privy should not be confused with The Old Priory, at Beechworth in Victoria, which is popular with humans but unsuitable for chooks on account of the high standard of cleanliness required.

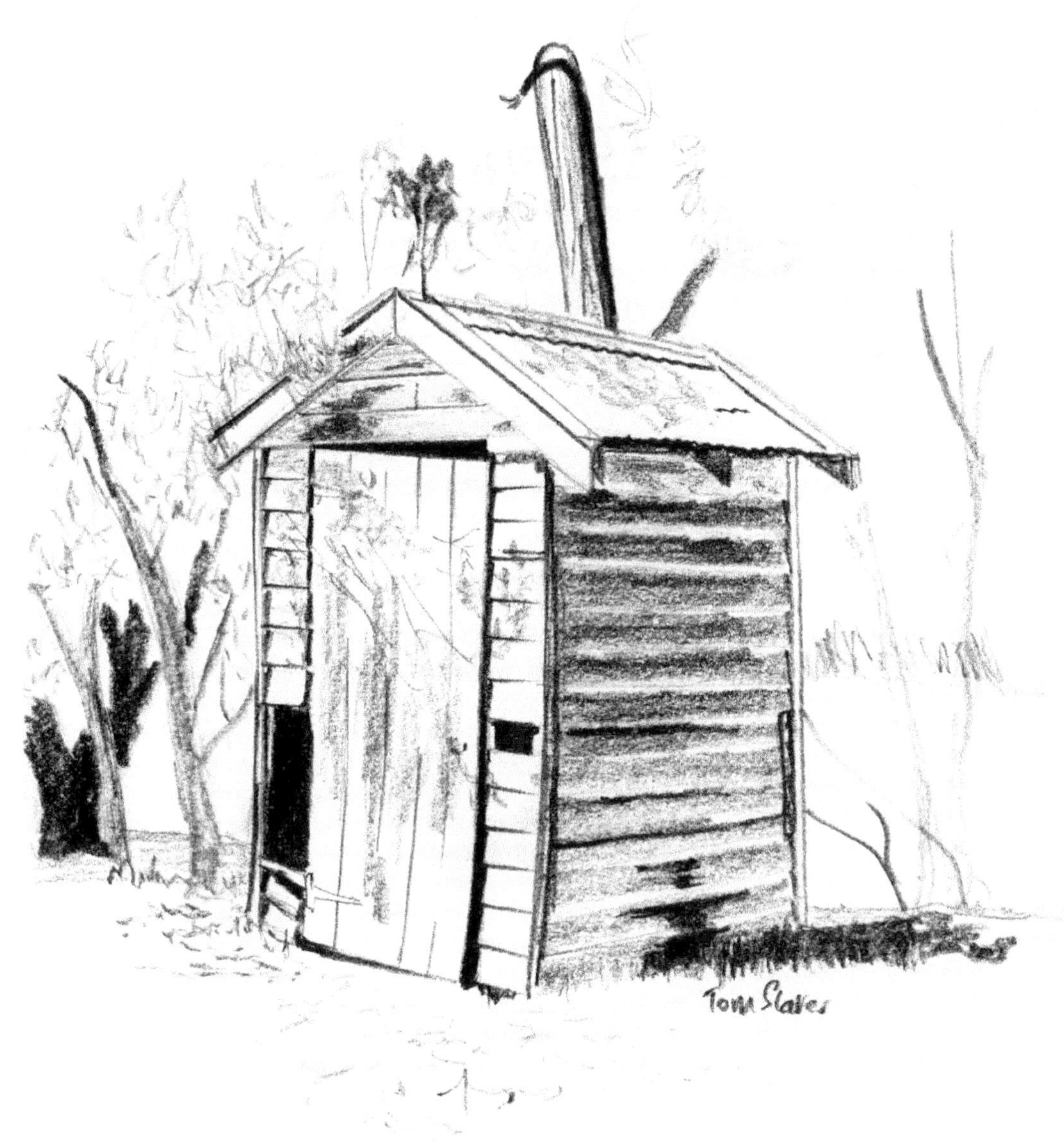
Tom Slaver

The Foundry, Fitzroy, Vic

This old iron foundry is an ideal base for the country chook keen to experience the delights and challenges of inner-city living. This truly unique chookotel, with its distinctly grimy atmosphere, blends the earthiness of a foundry with the up-market ambience of a modern inner city apartment area. Breathe deeply of the soot and heat in the late afternoon, head off to a local restaurant, and return when all is quiet in the evening.

At the time of publication this accommodation is unavailable, having been knocked down for new apartments. However the owners are looking to open new (that is, old) premises in another part of the city, and plan to open it for chook holidays. So watch for next year's *Good Chook Accommodation Guide*. In the meantime you can have a Virtual Iron Foundry holiday by purchasing the app, which is why we have included the demolished Foundry in this first edition.

Meanwhile, chickens looking for iron foundry accommodation will have to look overseas, as there is a shortage of such places in this country.

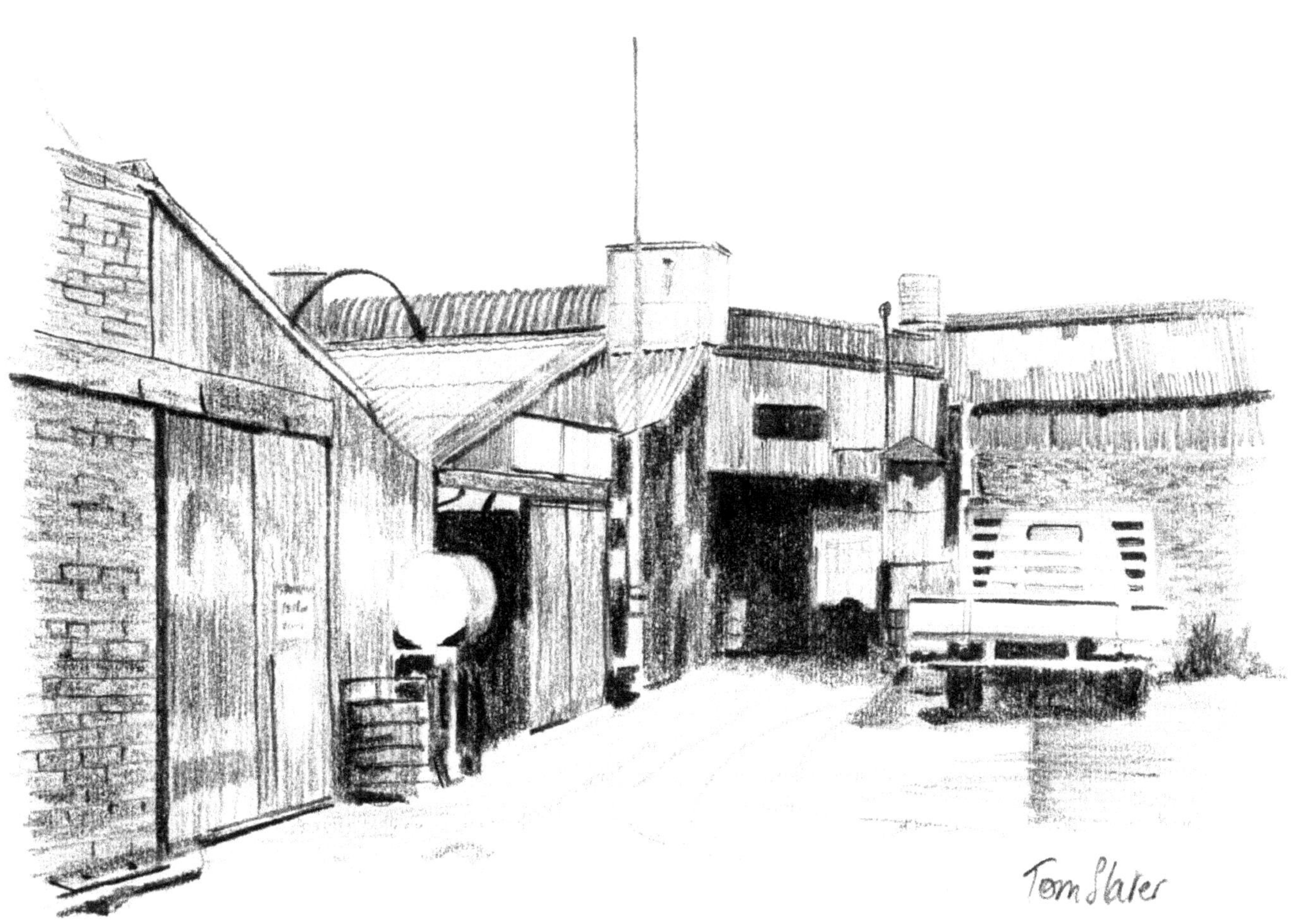
Tom Slater

The Tankstand, Shepparton, Vic

This beautiful old brick tankstand is just one of many eminent features of the William Orr campus of TAFE on the outskirts of Shepparton. Although, like the whole campus, it is kept clean and tidy, it still provides good accommodation if you pinch some straw from one of the sheds on the property. It's a great flapping-off point for visiting Shepparton's attractions, including the golf course and Furphy's Engineering, famous for the old Furphy water-carts. Reeves Lagoon, just down the road, is a breeding place for the chook-friendly ibis. The district's orchards are great scratching grounds, as are the Wm Orr paddocks close by. Fruit lovers can scavenge around the SPC factory across the river at Mooroopna.

Shepparton Golf Course is close by and welcomes visitors, but asks chickens to play at night, as their slower progress tends to hold up club members and other humans during the day. Chicken-sized golf clubs can be purchased at the Shepparton toy shop. Otherwise, just take a stroll around the course, which boasts many native plantations, thanks to the efforts of the legendary Royce Dickson.

(It was my privilege to work closely with Royce on the pilot 'Goulburn Valley Environmental Employment Program' in 1998-99. Royce's achievements in life – sporting, professional and as a community volunteer and environmentalist – after losing his favoured arm in an accident while working his first job, are so impressive that readers would be wondering if I was making it up. I mention him to somehow honour his memory, and for Maureen, the love of his life for over 60 years.)

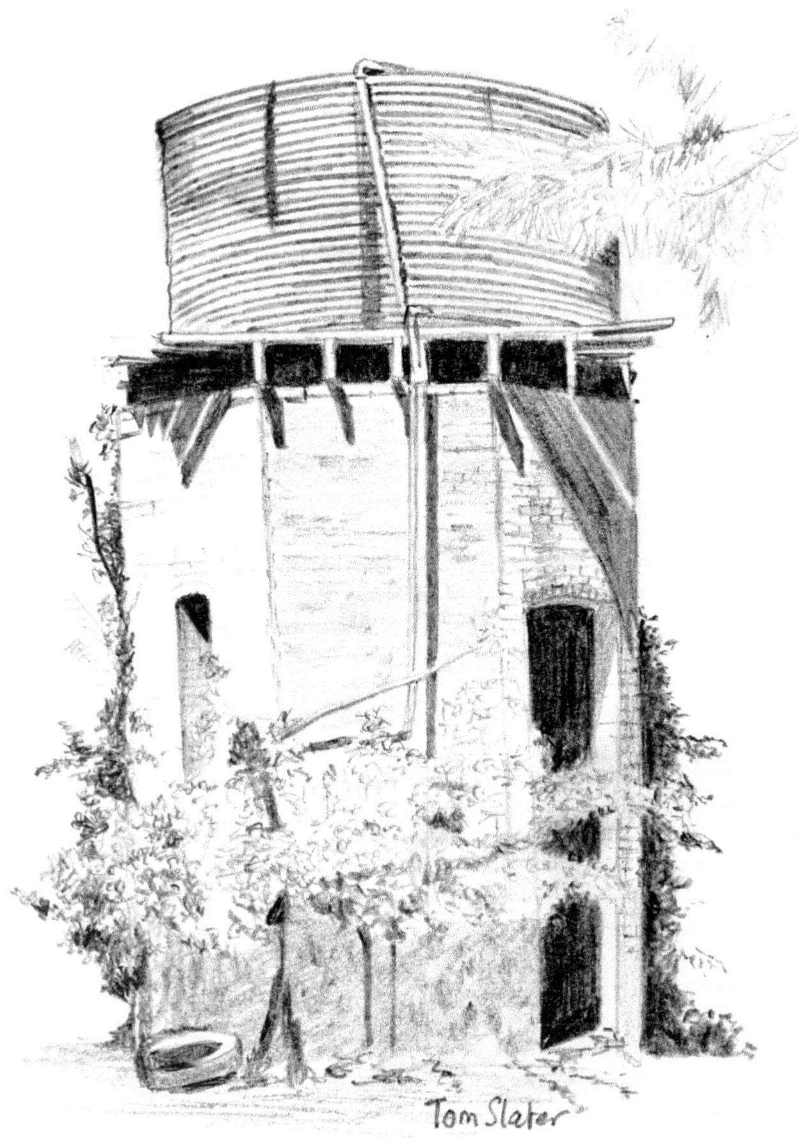
Tom Slater

The Manor House, Evandale, Tas

Don't be deceived by the fine architecture of this home in historic Evandale, Tasmania. In the rear garden the chicken-loving owners have maintained a run-down chook retreat with every comfort, including dust and spiders, a choice of grains and other produce in self-feeders, and ample perch space which eliminates the need for squabbles over the best perch. With a solid dog-proof fence and a no-cat policy, the owners have ensured a level of security that guarantees peace of mind to family groups with small chickens.

Evandale, situated handily between Launceston city and the airport, hosts an annual fair and penny-farthing cycle race. For several years the owners of The Manor House have offered a generous monetary prize for any four-chook team that manages to ride one of these cycles more than 3 metres without falling off. Unsurprisingly the prize has jackpotted every year, so your team could still be the first to win it.

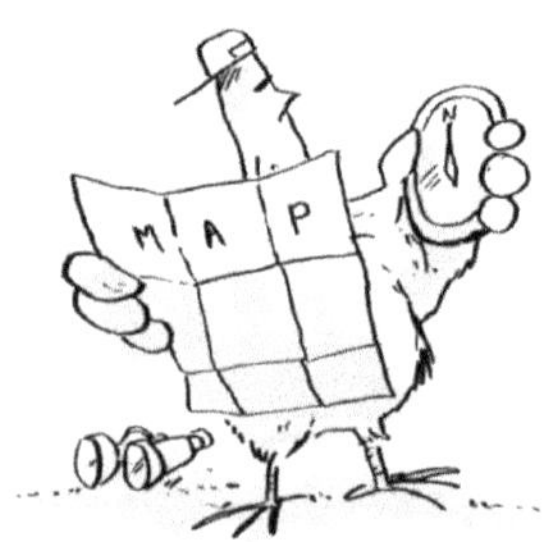

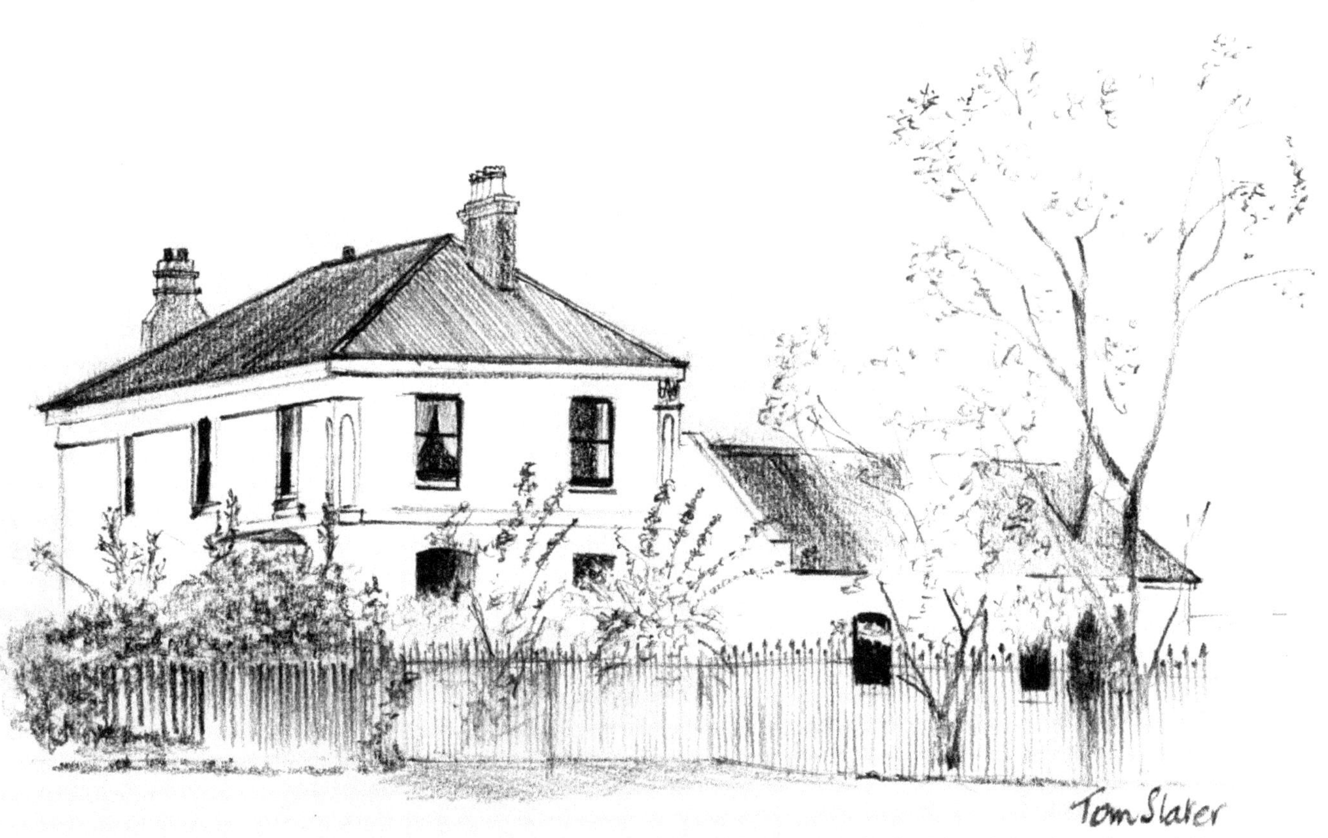
Tom Slater

Belair Station, SA

The first and most picturesque of the railway stations featured in this guide, Belair Station is in the Adelaide Hills. It features a long curving platform, and is on the interstate route from Adelaide to Melbourne. One goods shed has been set aside for chook accommodation. The Overland train twice a week does not take poultry as passengers, but the goods van provides sufficient comfort. It will stop at Belair if you pull the emergency cord at the critical time, but be quick to disembark without being seen as penalties apply. Chooks with business in Adelaide favour this location, for obvious reasons, returning home each night to roost in the comfort of the shed.

The author, born and raised in Adelaide himself, had a cousin who lived at Belair South, but as this is of no interest to anybody, please disregard the information.

It is sometimes thought that Belair was named after the Chevrolet Bel-Air, but since it was named 100 years before the Chev, this seems unlikely. Anyway Gustav Ludewigs, who may have named Belair, never owned a Chev.

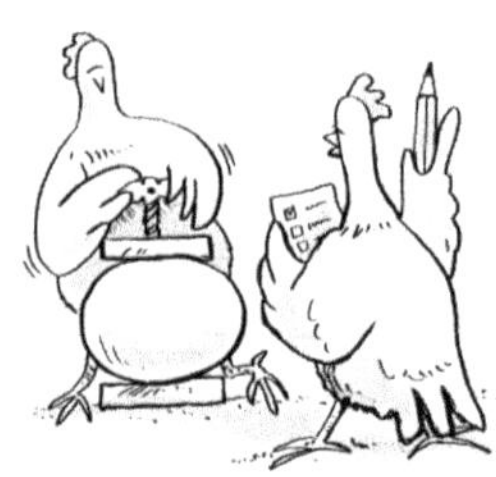

According to Harvard University, taking the ultimate compressional strength of egg shell material to be about 170x106 N/m2, the diameter of a 'large' chicken egg to be about 1.75" and the typical shell thickness around 0.023", then the cross-sectional area of the shell wall is approximately 1/8 sq in, or 8x10-5 m2 which, when combined with the ultimate strength, theoretically *will support a 1.4x104 N load (3,000 lbs). But I suggest it is still not a good idea to stand on your eggs. By the way, how do you measure the diameter of an egg?*

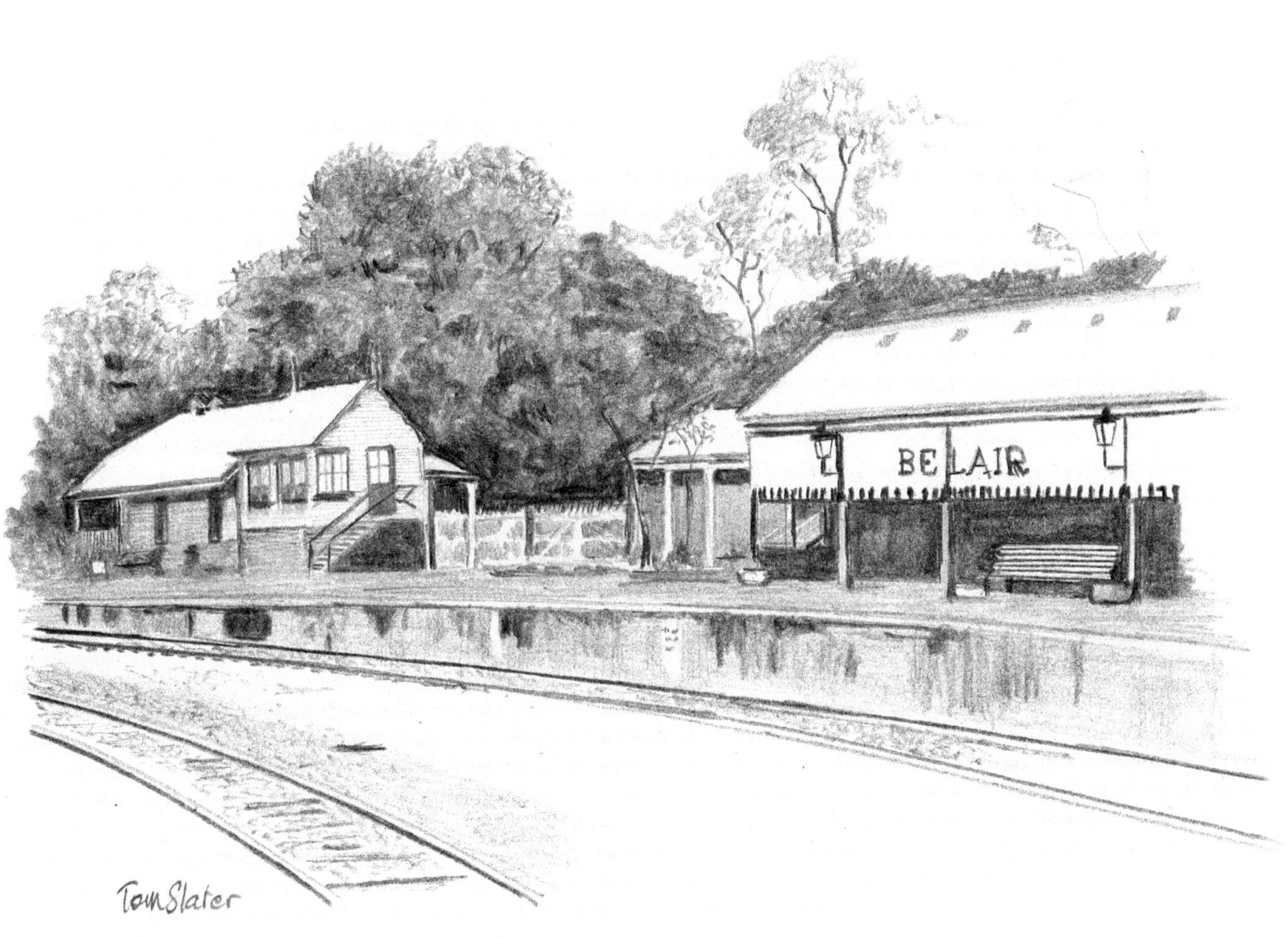
BELAIR
Tom Slater

Hobart Central, Tas

Now here's a real surprise packet. Only five minutes flap and run from the city centre, this attractive cottage boasts a warm under-house area suitable for several families at a time. The ideal location for a weekend in town, or for a longer stay.

With no dogs allowed you can let the chicks run free. However like most of Hobart the block is very steep, and is not suitable for chooks with mobility issues. Interstate visitors are welcome but quarantine restrictions may apply. Check with your Department of Agriculture or your local veterinary service. If in doubt, some Border Force officials will turn a blind eye if you slip them a fresh egg, so be prepared to lay at short notice.

The Australian Antarctic Division ships can often be seen at the Hobart Wharf. However care is required when visiting, as a chook once failed to disembark after a tour, and was not discovered for a week, and then only because an engineer found six eggs in a corner of the engine room.

Forced to winter in the Antarctic, the hen became the Guinness Book of Records' longest surviving domestic hen below the 66th parallel. Sadly it did not survive to return to its home coop, and the record was awarded posthumously. A memorial to The Anonymous Hen was erected at Casey base. When the news got back to Australia there was an outpouring of grief, and supermarkets recorded a sharp fall in the purchase of frozen chickens which lasted for several months.

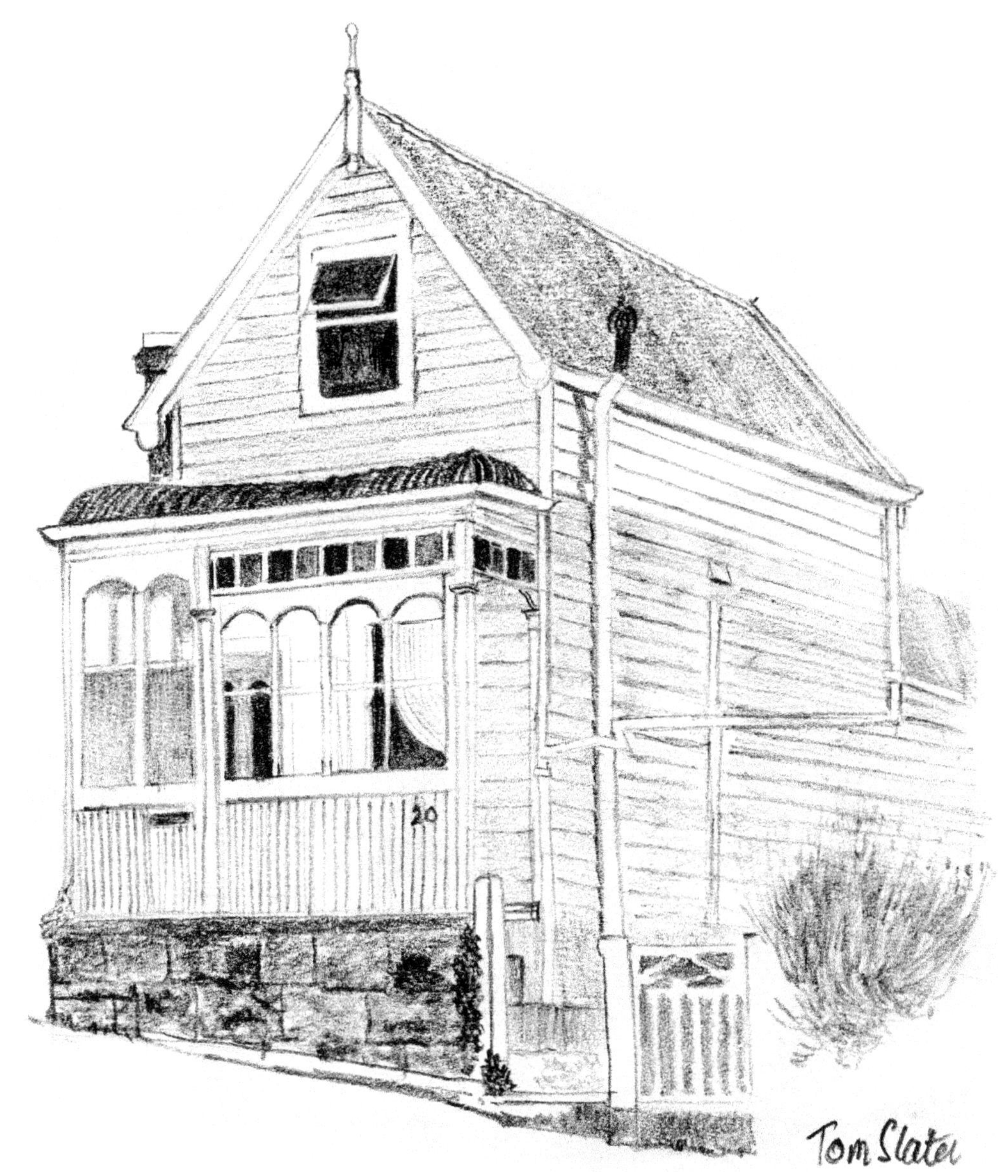
20
Tom Slater

The Beechworth School, Vic

Exclusive accommodation is available in the shelter shed at the historic Beechworth Primary School. Bookings may be made with the caretaker. The historic town of Beechworth has many historic attractions, including the historic police station, the historic old gaol, the historic court house, and many other historic features of historical interest.

Interested in the history of North East Victoria? Look no further. Chooks are not encouraged in the main street but there are plenty of other places to drop into, or for that matter to leave your droppings. You can lunch at the Old Beechworth Bakery, but some chooks may find the sight of chicken sandwiches disturbing. Only available in school holidays.

A visit to picturesque Yackandandah is well worth the effort. Yackandandah is a small town, but still quite a lot bigger than Yacka, north of Adelaide on the Main North Rd, which is why its name is so much longer. At the time of writing, the temperature in Yackandandah is 18 deg. C, and the wind 8kph. A good time to book.

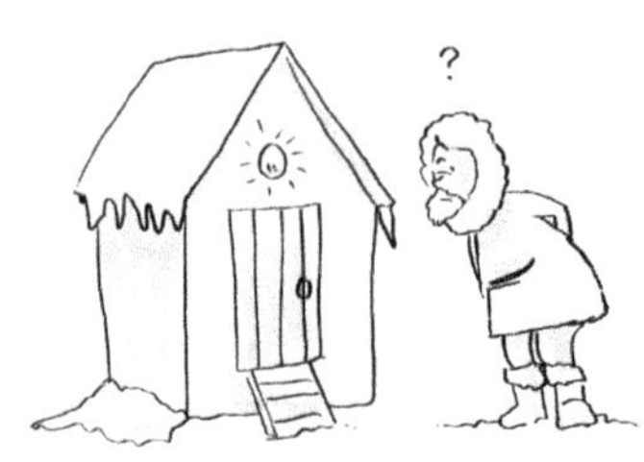

There is an automatic battery operated chicken coop door on the market, with a timer and a light sensor, which apparently works at temperatures as low as -10degC. What a relief it must be for the legions of chicken owners who hate the sight of chickens, live in the world's frigid zones, don't bother collecting their eggs or have trouble telling the time.

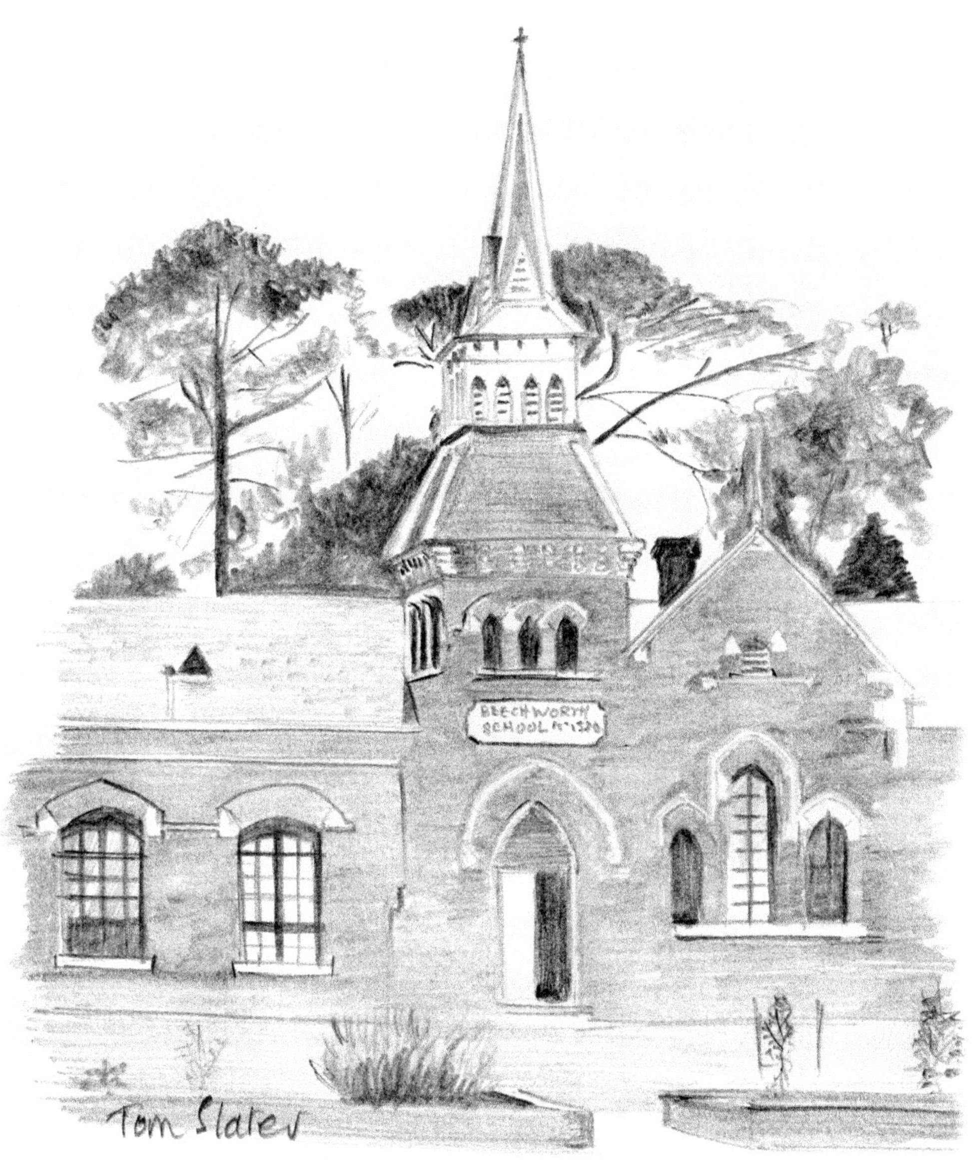
BEECHWORTH
SCHOOL No 1520
Tom Slater

Busselton Cemetery, WA

It's not everyone's cup of tea, nor every chicken's pot of bran and pollard either. But the old Busselton cemetery has some great attractions. Chooks have free access to the old peppercorn trees, which provide great roosts safe from mongrel dogs.

In this peaceful environment you can sun yourself on a comfortable slab or in the grass, and for the historically minded chook there is endless interest in reading the headstones. With memorials of all shapes and sizes there is plenty to sketch if you can handle a pen or pencil. This is budget accommodation at its best.

Each school holidays, the City of Busselton Youth Team runs events and activities for youth to participate in. It is planned to offer activities for chooks in future school holidays.

Busselton is in Noongar country, which covers the entire southwest of Western Australia. It has been the land of the Noongar people for 45,000 years. This is possibly not of interest to chooks, but it sure should be of interest to other Australians.

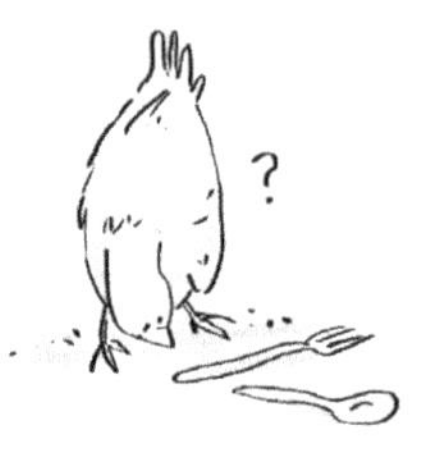

A common mistake is to talk about someone 'laying down'. This is always incorrect. People lie *down. Hens don't lay down either. They either lay, or they lie down. In any case you would think only ducks could lay down, and they don't either. There are two exceptions. First, someone might 'lay down the law', but in this case the verb is transitive, so that's different. Second someone else might 'lay the table'. There is no recorded instance of a hen laying a table of any size.*

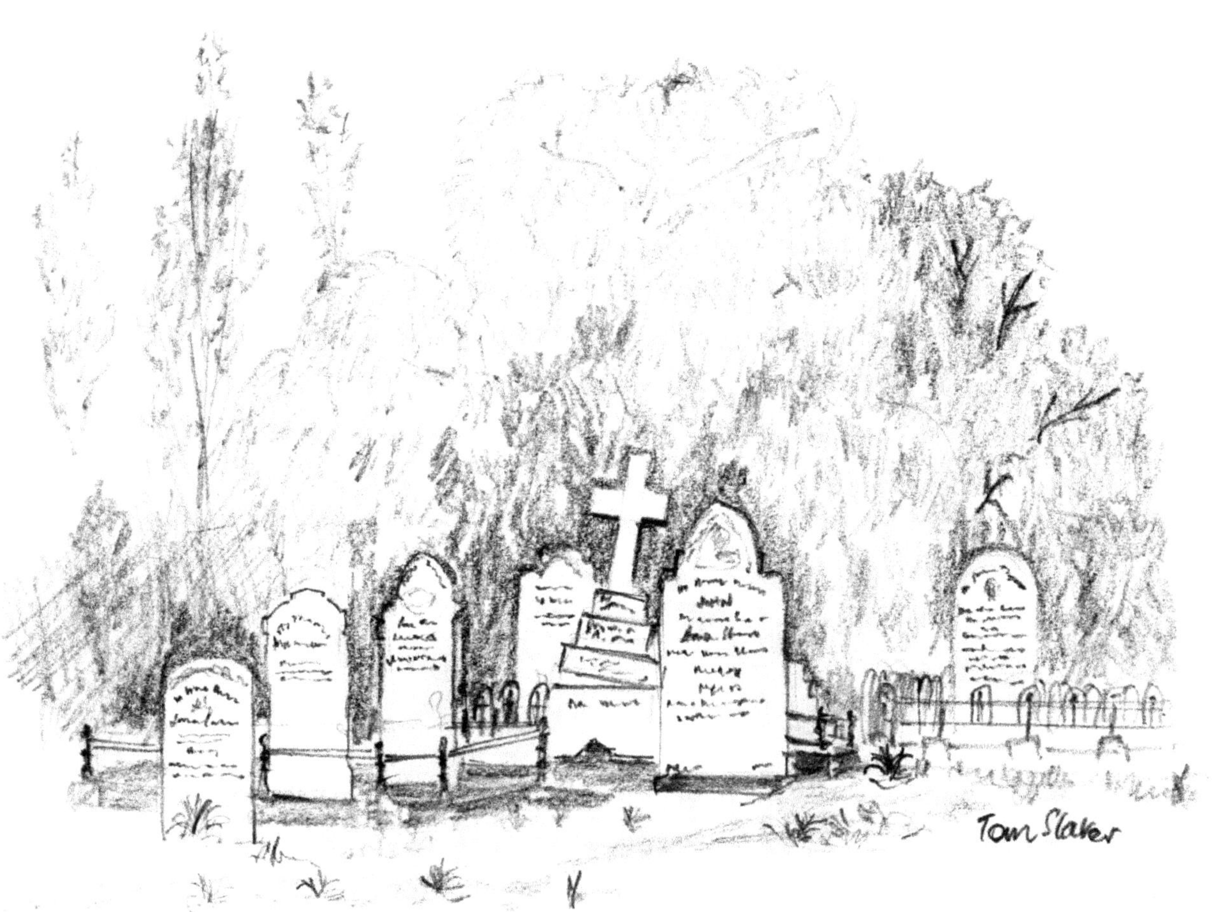
Tom Slater

Shepherd's Hut, Rawnsley Park, SA

Located in the Flinders Ranges, just south of Wilpena Pound, Shepherd's Hut is a home away from home for the well-to-do chook. Located on the Rawnsley Park Station (sheep, not railway – the nearest railway is… oh, don't worry) – the buildings exude historic charm.

Explore your surrounds, whether the old homestead and outbuildings or the wide open spaces abounding in worms and insects. On windy days simply retreat to the hut and have a good old scratch around in the old fireplace, sharpening your beak and ingesting useful carbon in the process. Your health will improve in a week.

On Tuesday evenings check out the Happy Hour at the on-site tourist park and pick up free scraps from the barbecues.

The name Rawnsley comes from Rawnsley Bluff, an impressive peak on the southern rim of Wilpena Pound. The bluff was named after HC Rawnsley who arrived from England under false pretences claiming to be a surveyor. He was a man 'of dubious skill and experience'. It is not recommended that chooks attempt the climb up the bluff, as there is a dearth of food outlets on the trek.

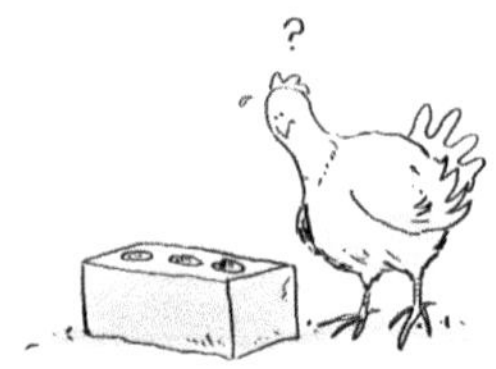

A dozen large eggs at the supermarket are supposed to weigh at least 700 grams, though my chooks lay much bigger eggs than that. Still even their largest eggs, around 100 grams, don't rate compared to the weight of a house brick, which is approx. 3.1 kg. This might explain why hens don't lay house bricks.

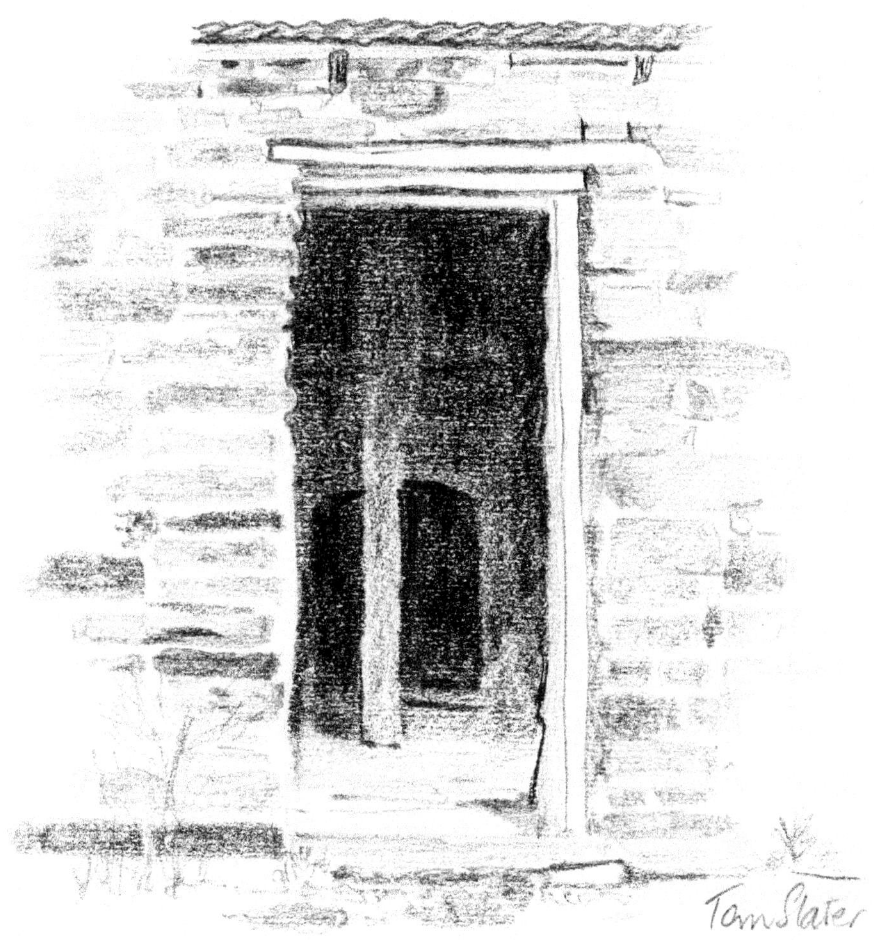
Tom Slater

Thatches for Scratchers, Vic

Located at Winiam East in Victoria's Wimmera region, Thatches for Scratchers is one of the most comfortable and stylish chookotels in Australia. Visitors make themselves at home anywhere in the straw at the back of the shed. Great smells from the thatched roof down, including old cow manure. Excellent views through all the gaps. Our advice is to do what you do best – scratch. Then make yourself a good dust bath, sit back and think about the good old days when the grain silo at the back was full of wheat.

Local attractions include The Little Desert, and the local wind farm, which was the first to develop the new sport of chicken-winging, which has really taken off. On certain windy days and in certain specific locations, chooks can spread their wings and get an exciting lift off the ground from the updraft. To date the record altitude achieved stands at 45 metres, but practice is required to ensure a safe landing from such heights. A bit of practice leaping off elevated perches before your holiday is advised.

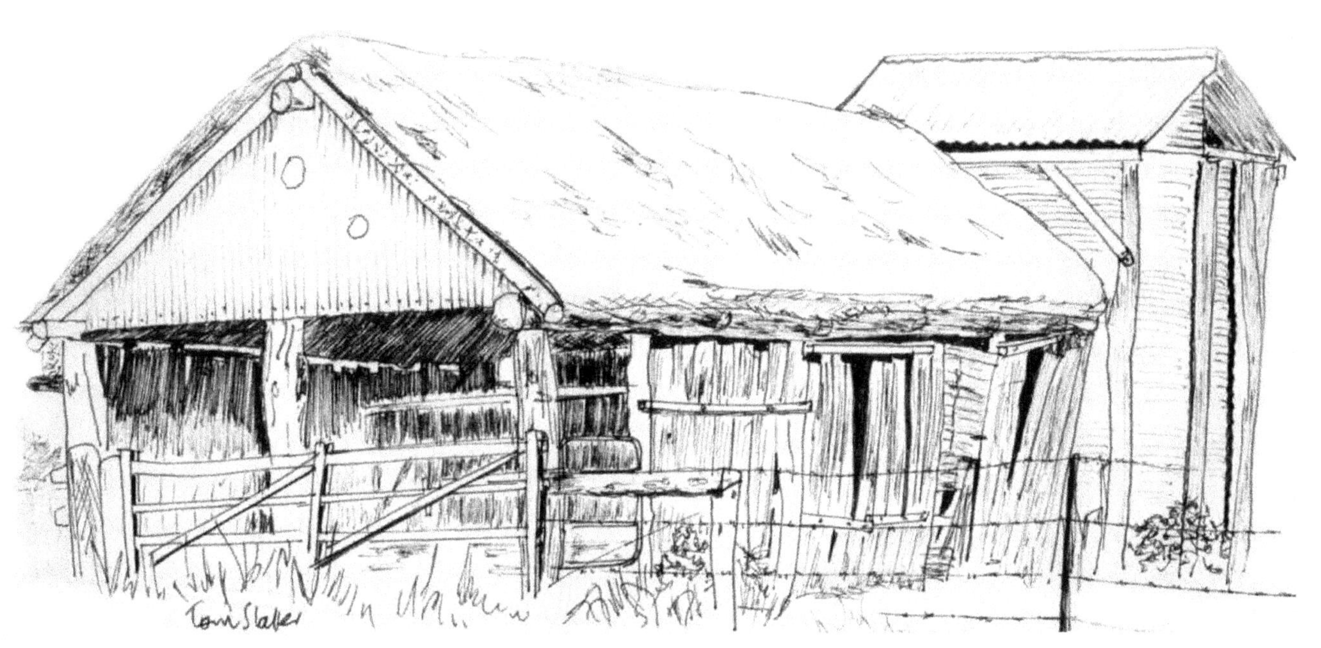
Tom Slater

The Lock-up, Barrow Creek, NT

This unusual accommodation is at the old telegraph station at Barrow Creek in the Northern Territory. It is the most remote place listed in this directory, but not the most inaccessible. Being situated on the Stuart Highway between Alice Springs and Darwin, rides are readily available to hitch-hikers. Many chooks catch The Ghan in Adelaide, get off at Alice Springs and use a wing to wave down a road-train or ute heading north.

Study the history of the old telegraph line, or fossick for gold amongst the surrounding rocks, then relax over some bran and pollard at the hotel, and watch the stars before retiring for the night.

We are told that one of the most momentous events at Barrow Creek was the opening of the store and the existing hotel in 1932. This occurred just in time to take advantage of the gold rush to Tennant Creek the following year. This gives me an excuse to mention that my father and his mate Bruce Clezy staffed the first (ES&A) bank in Tennant Creek the following year. Made of corrugated iron, it was claimed to be the only bank in the world with a dirt floor, so I imagine it would have been the preferred bank for the local chooks, though Dad never mentioned that.

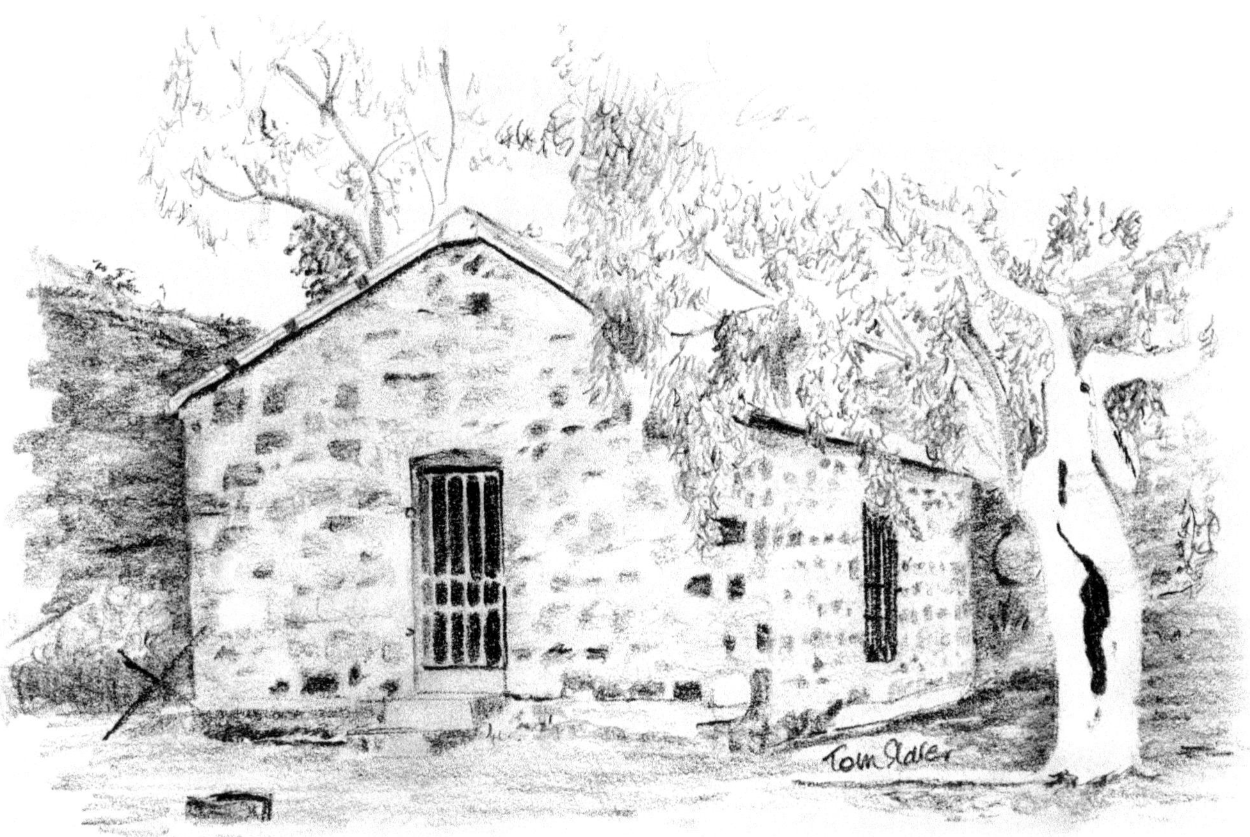

The Ruin, Quorn, SA

Situated just out of Quorn on the road to Port Augusta, this superb ruin offers unbeatable value for the budget-minded hen who is happy to take along a good watch-dog to protect from foxes, and a piece of roofing to keep out the weather. A fire may be lit in one of the attractive fireplaces for extra warmth in the evening, while the surrounding paddocks will reward the dedicated scavenger with a variety of organic treats during the day.

It is advisable to take your own transport, as The Ruin does not have a shuttle bus or hire out vehicles. Towns such as Quorn (see elsewhere) are full of attractions. In particular the historic Pichi Richi Railway running from Quorn to Port Augusta (and back) operates on selected days between March and November. It is possible to take the train from Quorn, take a flying leap near The Ruin, then saunter back to your digs. But don't forget you may have left the car in Quorn.

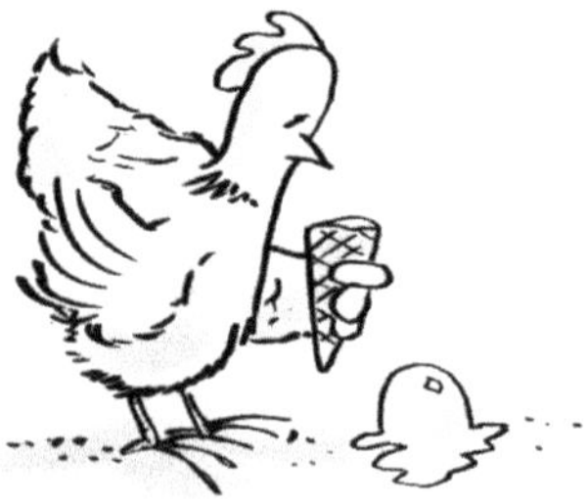

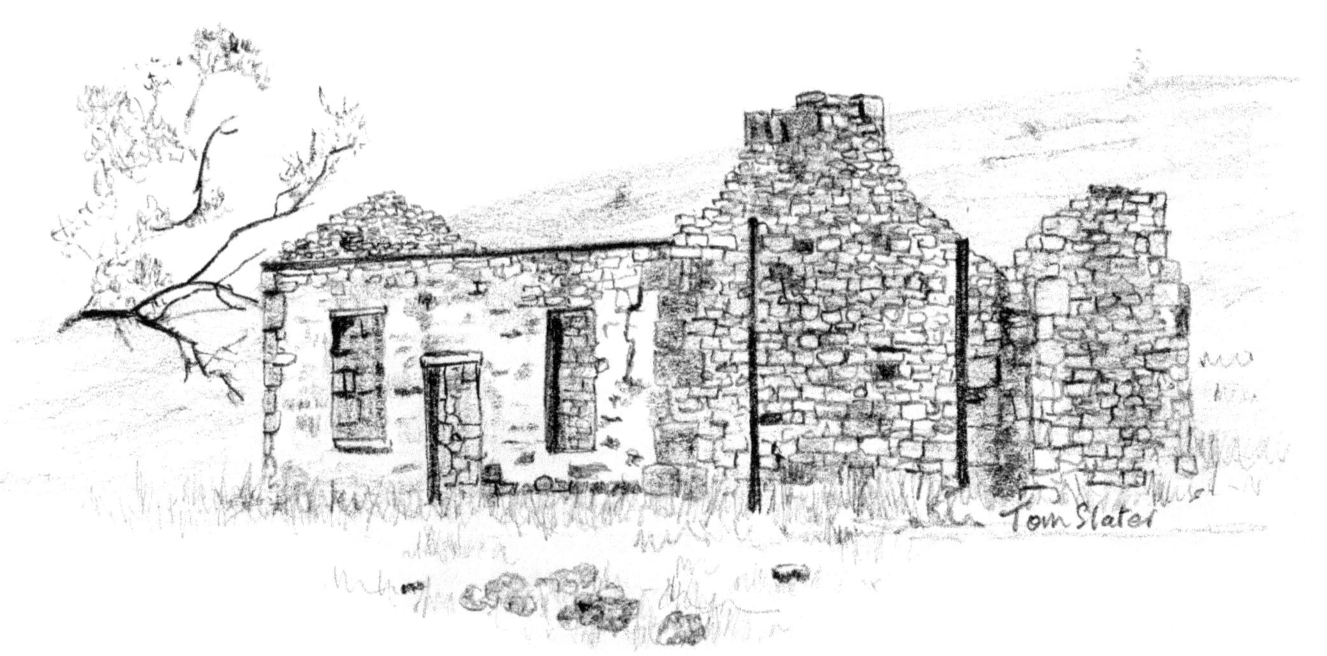
Tom Slater

The Riley, Watsons Bay, NSW

Although no longer in its heyday as a dusty and decrepit old car in a suburban shed, this restored Riley nevertheless has a certain charm, and there is nothing like the smell of leather upholstery, even to members of the poultry family. One feature of this particular unit is that the owner is willing to locate the unit at various points of the property if so desired. Otherwise, simply occupy it inside the shed and enjoy the extra security of the roll-a-door.

Potential hirers are advised however that unusual (for chooks) restrictions apply, and significant additional fees apply for dirty footmarks and errant droppings and the like. Interstate travellers can take a train from the airport or Central Station to Circular Quay, then board the Watsons Bay ferry. It's then just a short flap or strut to the The Riley.

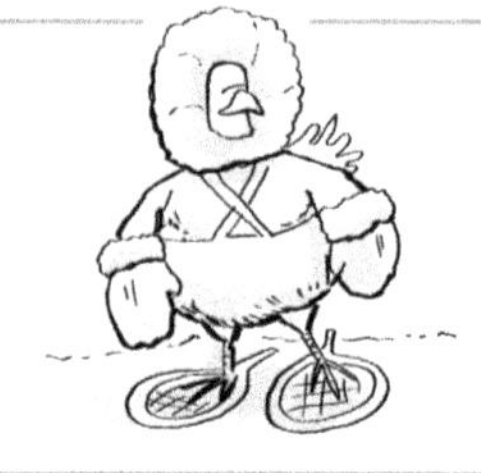

There have been no known sightings of chickens in the Antarctica since the last Ice Age, and even before that.

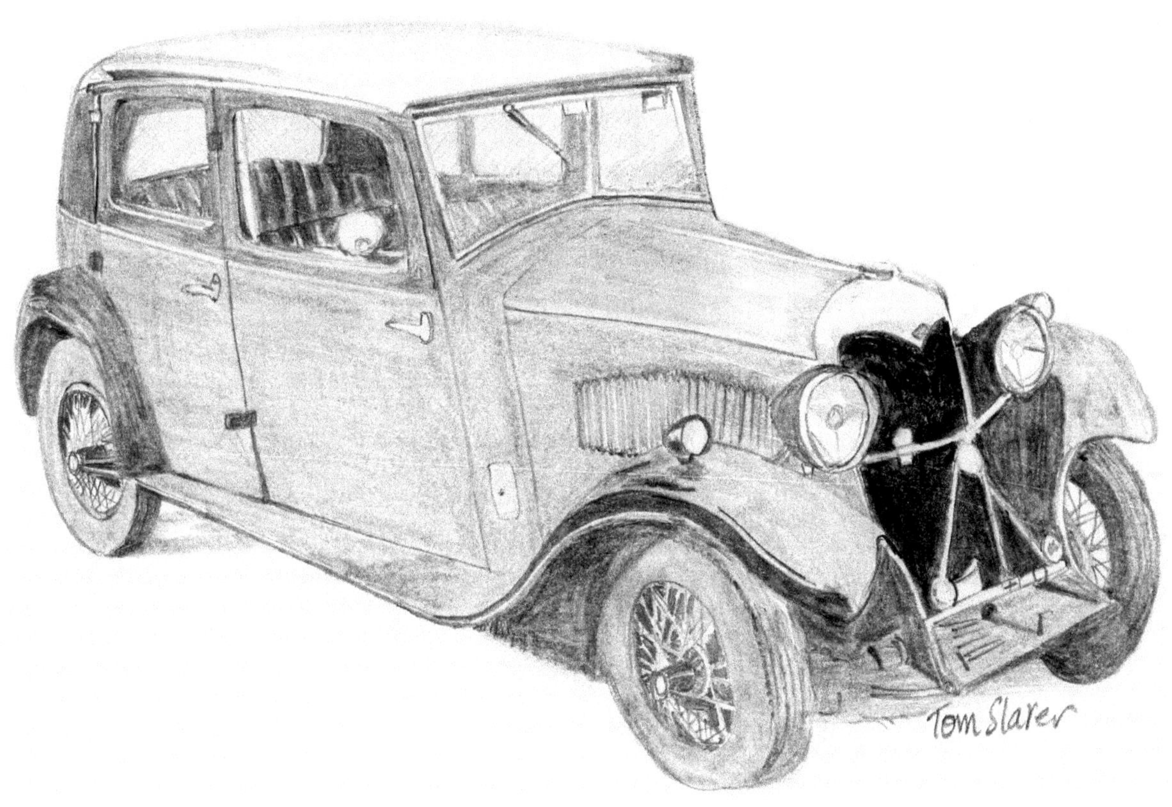
Tom Slater

Riverside Retreat, NSW (or Vic)

Riverside Retreat stands close to the bank of the Murray River. As for The Privy (described earlier), the location is not certain until you find it. Once found, however, Riverside Retreat proves to be one of the most attractive shed-style chook accommodations in the country, featuring homely vertical slats and second-hand corrugated iron to make any country chook feel at home. A short flapping run takes you to a nearby vineyard, where endless entertainment is provided in the summer watching cockatoos and other pest birds take off in alarm at the scare-guns protecting the grapes.

While the attractions of Echuca and Moama are widely recognised, it is a little-known fact that there is a fortnightly public horse sale auction at the Echuca District Livestock Exchange. An increasing number of country chooks are attending these sales, purchasing draught horses to pull the increasingly popular chook-wagons travelling the back roads of Australia.

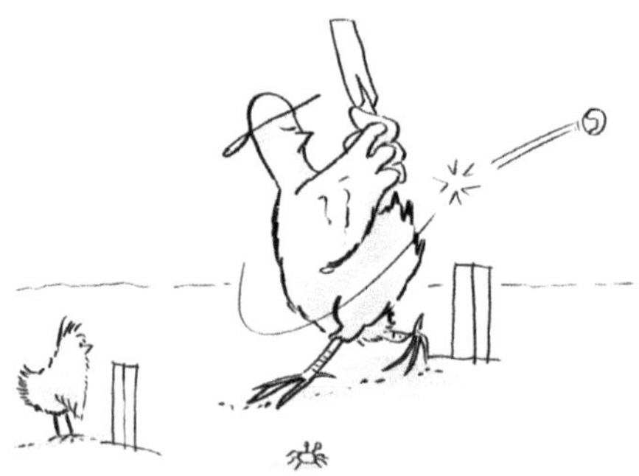

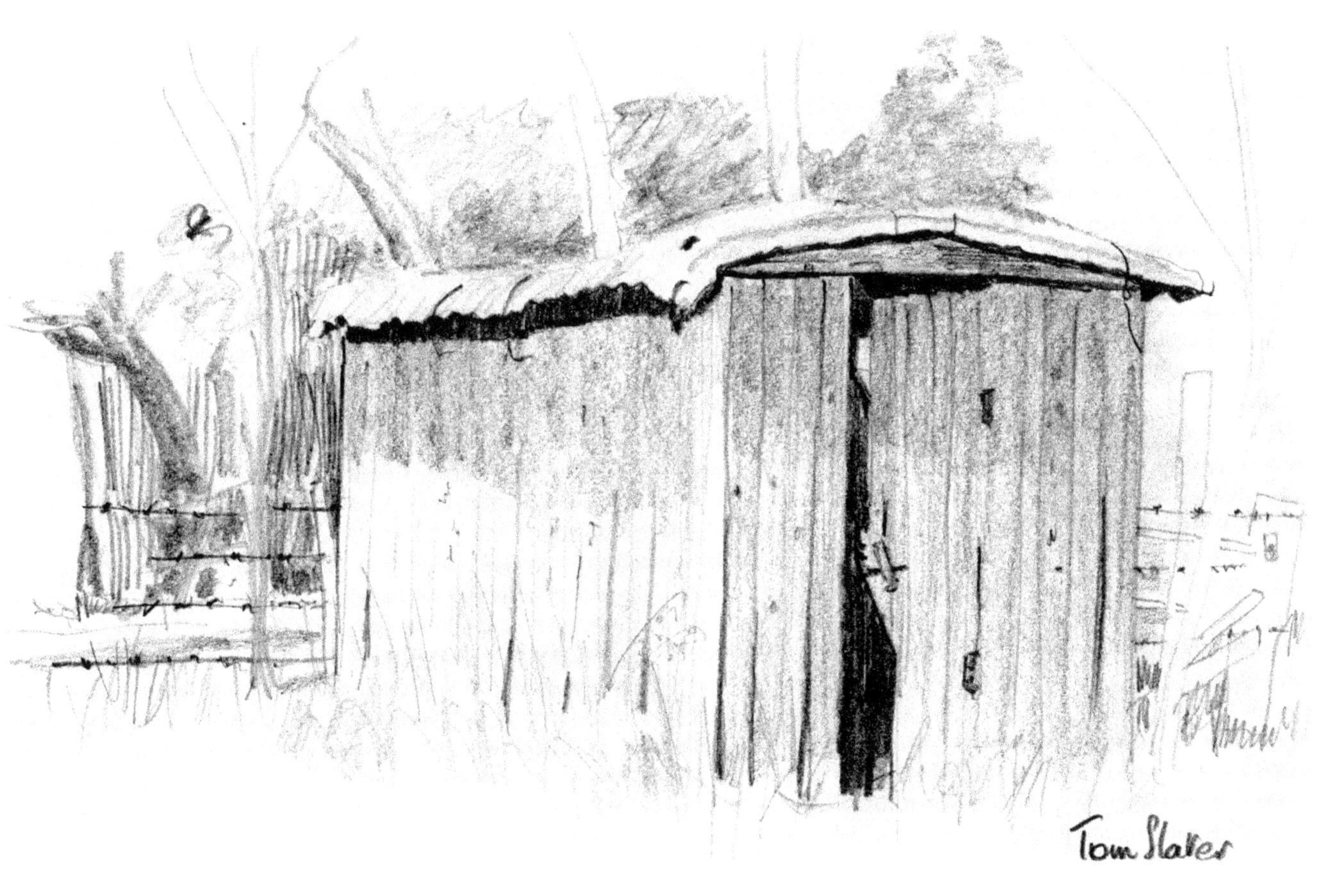
Tom Slater

Hawkestowe Park, Vic

Hawkestowe Park is a historic property on the Plenty River, on the northern outskirts of Melbourne. Managed by Parks Victoria, it has a tenuous connection, through one of the early owners, with Swallow and Ariel Biscuits. This is obviously of little interest to the holidaying chook, especially as biscuit crumbs are rarely found, except after visitors, particularly at the weekends.

The old buildings are in such a state of repair as to inspire awe and confidence, but again the visiting chook will be more interested in the variety of accommodation available, ranging from bush settings to domestic settings in wooden or stone sheds. Old machinery has been strategically placed as viewing perches for the use of guest poultry.

As a matter of interest, Hawkestowe Park was not named after former Prime Minister Bob Hawke, whose toe was never seen in the park. Neither is it connected, as is sometimes thought, with the Hawkesbury River, which bears a superficial resemblance to the nearby Plenty River in that they both have flowing water.

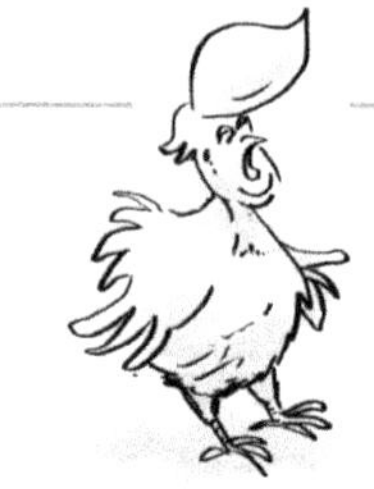

There are no free range chickens on Donald Trump's golf courses. And there are no chicken coops in Trump Tower.

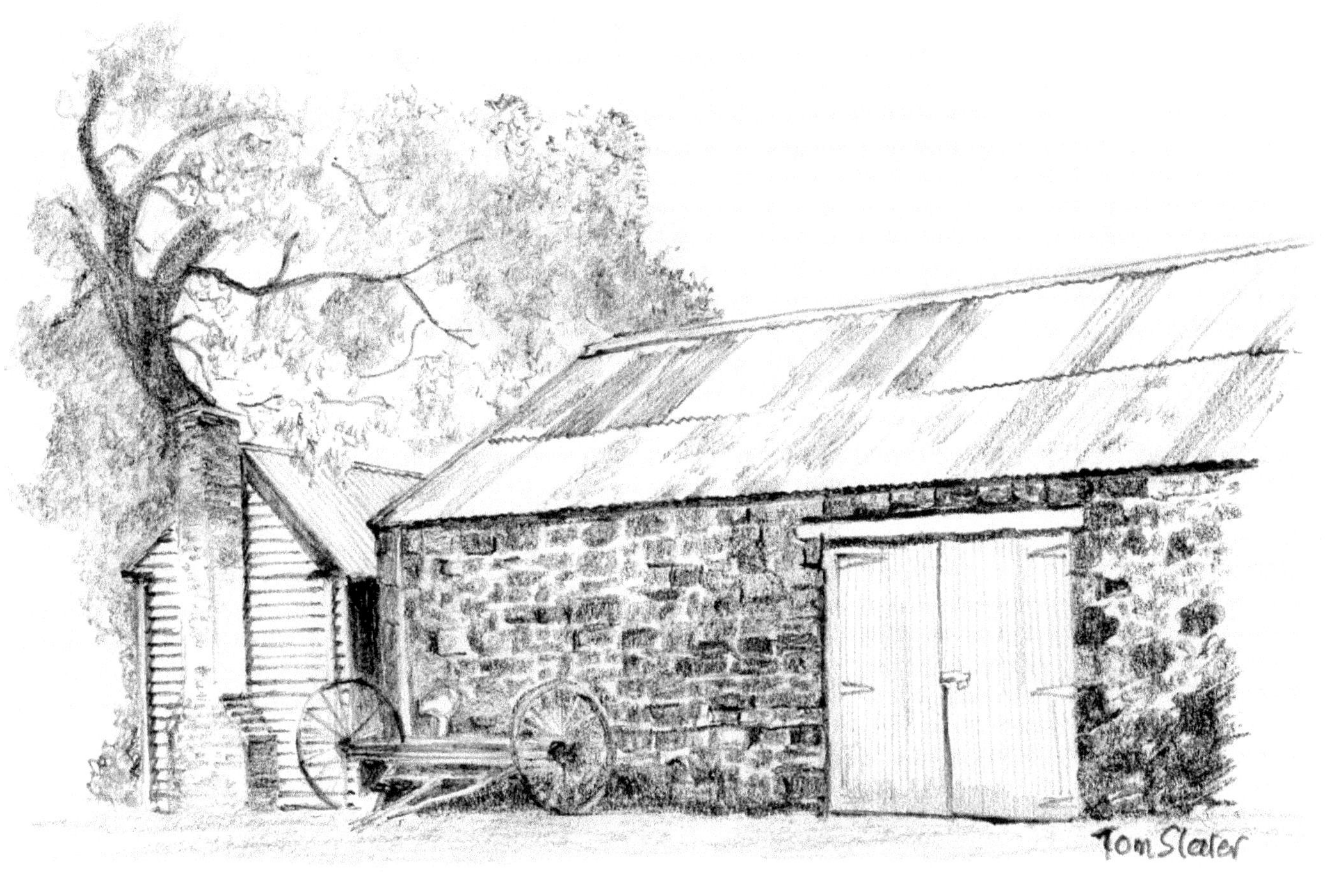
Tom Slater

Old Vehicle Shed, Bungaree Station, South Australia

Bungaree Station in the Clare Valley in SA was voted Book-a-Chook's most popular holiday destination in 2019. And little wonder. Established in 1841, the property and its owners have been an integral part of the SA pastoral industry from earliest days.

There is a great range of attractions within the bounds of the station. You need to book in advance before you leave home to ensure you have a place to stay. The old vehicle shed has several classes of accommodation ranging from the President's Suite in the old truck cabin to the back of an old hay cart, and several in between.

For the adventurous, you can ask to sleep out under the stars during the high season of summer, but it is advisable to bring your own perch, or hire one at the Farmers' Store in the nearby Clare township.

Every part of Bungaree is impressive – the property's own church, the Store, the Shearing Shed, the magnificent homestead itself, the shearer's quarters and much more.

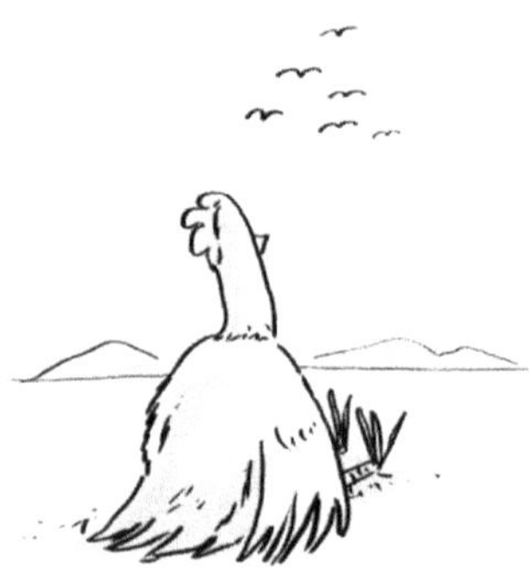

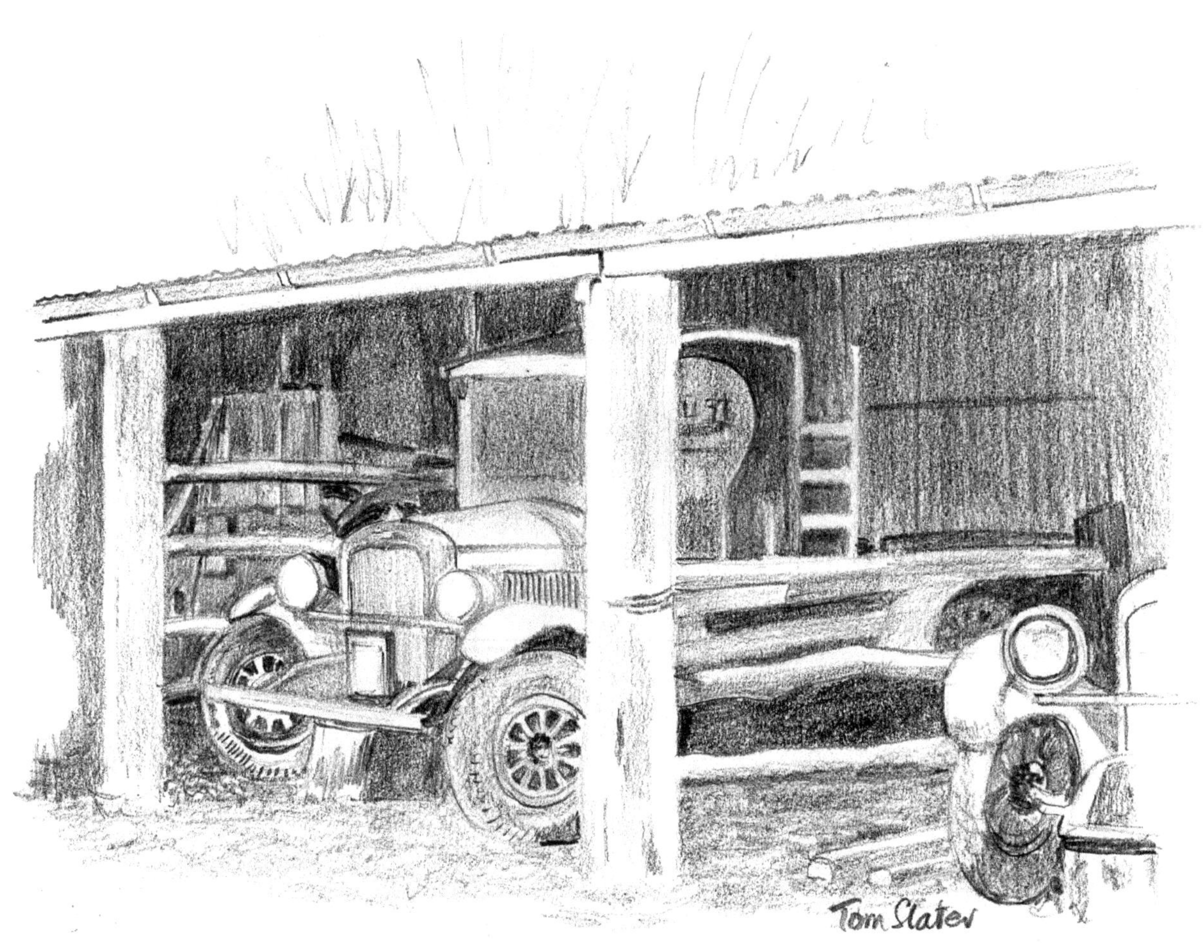
Tom Slater

The Old Post Office, Busselton, WA

Location, location! The Old Post Office Café in Busselton is one of the best located first class chook stay-overs in the West, situated on the corner of Queen Street and Marine Terrace, just one block away from the foreshore and an easy walk to the famous Busselton Jetty, which is almost 2 kms long.

This is a highly sought-after destination for the hen looking for a break from city life and cooking. You can spend lazy days at the beach – no need to swim – and saunter back to your quarters for a meal delivered to your coop by the café's resident chef. Seniors' discounts are available on meals and accommodation for chooks over 8 years of age (which of course means they are rarely able to be taken advantage of). Unfair? That's the market place. You can always shop around – like you do for banks and aged care providers.

May 4 is International Respect for Chickens Day, and May is International Respect for Chickens Month, according to United Poultry Concerns, based in Machipongo, VA.

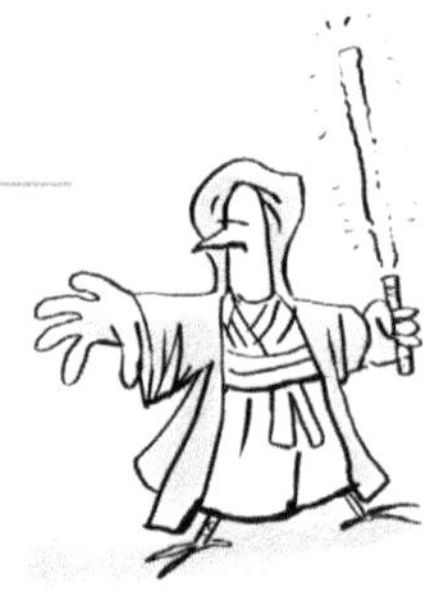

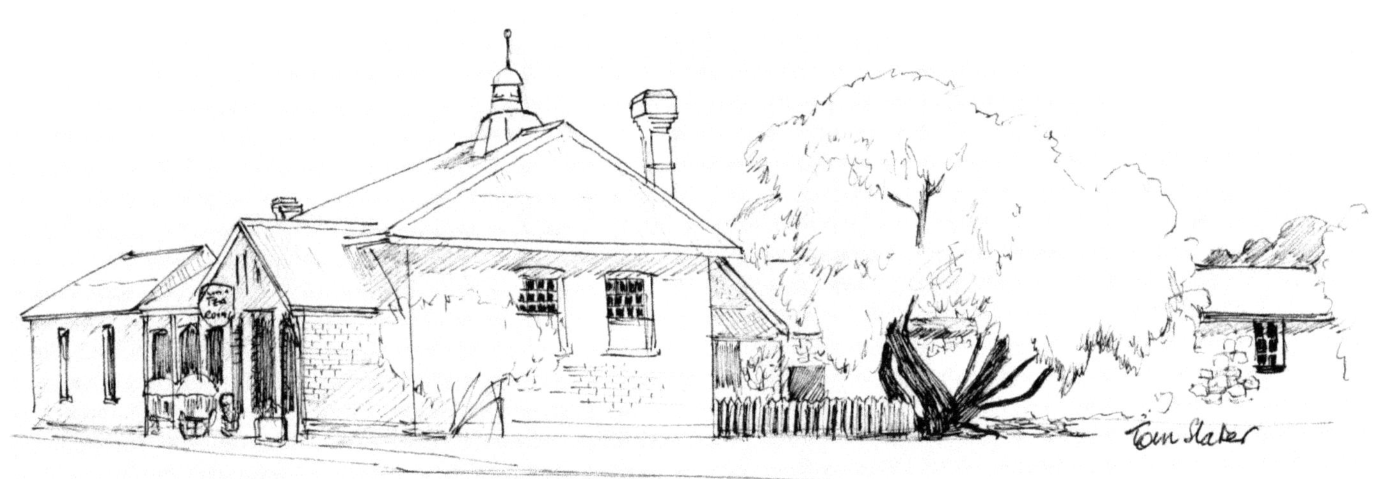
Tom Slater

Lulu at Calulu, Vic

This stone farmhouse with walls half a metre thick is at Calulu in East Gippsland. The property boasts an ideal chook-shed for a holiday. Originally built for chooks, it lay idle for some years while the owners battled Indian Mynahs that pinched the feed, not to mention droughts and flooding rains. These days it offers farm stays for city chooks, though chooks from dry farming areas will love the change of scene. Day trips down to the nearby Mitchell River can be arranged, as well as excursions to Boggy Creek, Dirty Hollow, Wuk Wuk and Briagalong.

Onsite attractions include an aviary exhibiting canaries, finches, quail and other small birds. Many of the smaller breeds of bantams have found that an hour spent here among these tiny birds has boosted their self-image, and many return to Lulu year after year for a confidence boost.

A unique attraction at Lulu is Bo, a boof-headed cattle dog who will chase sticks, tennis balls, or anything else all day, just as long as some equally indefatigable human will throw them. His most spectacular habit is to leap into bushes and attempt to climb trees if he knows the prize is there.

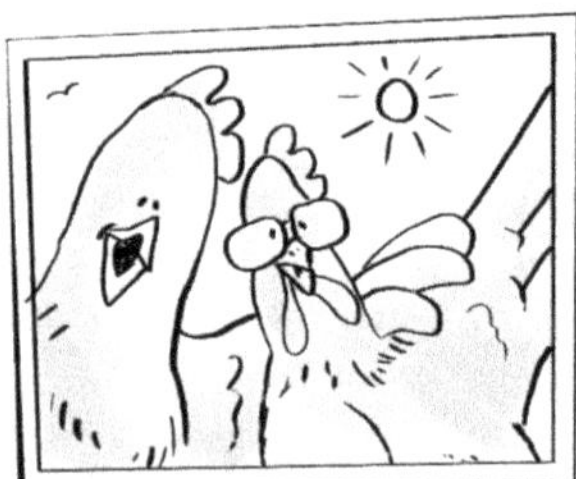

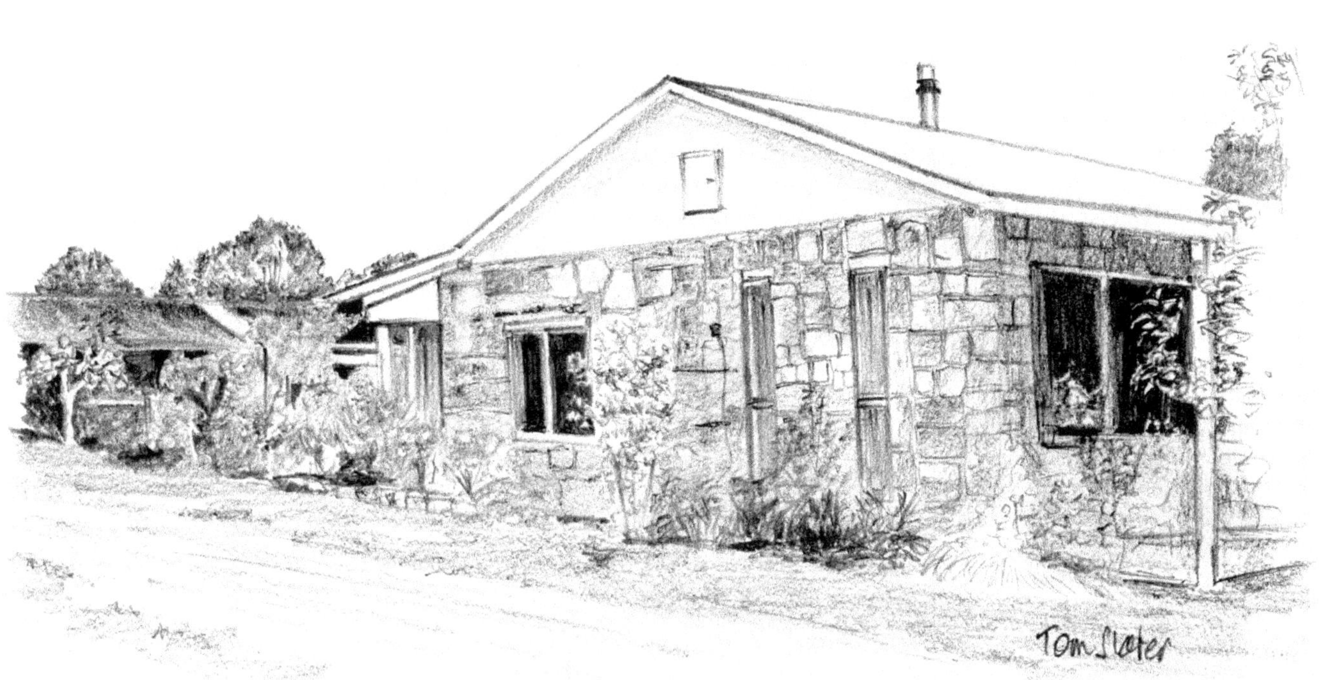
Tom Slater

The Coop, Kingston Beach, Tas

Hidden away behind this imposing residence right on the foreshore at Kingston Beach is The Coop, a dilapidated chook-house which is deemed to have great heritage value. Apart from that, the major attraction of this popular venue is the situation.

A leisurely scratch and poke about in a southerly direction finds you looking out towards The Iron Pot lighthouse at the mouth of the Derwent River. Look back to the north and see Mount Wellington towering over the city of Hobart. A great take-off point for exploring places like Tinderbox, Lower Snug, Turnip Fields, or the rubbish tip near Knocklofty (see *RACV Road Atlas of Australia* 2nd edition map 228 B3 for tip location).

A bus from the city stops right outside, and the local hairdresser just around the corner caters for wing-clips, feather trims, perms and even pedicures, manicures being obviously irrelevant to chooks.

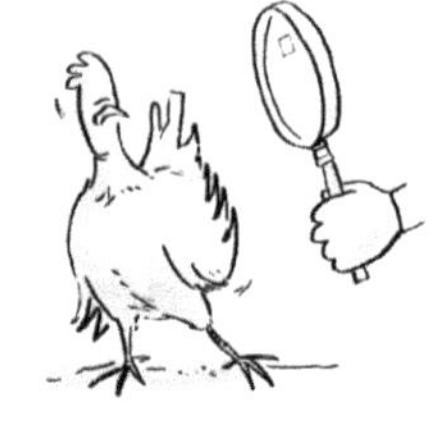

'The easiest anatomy of the chicken to assess is the external anatomy.' (From an academic article titled The Anatomy and Physiology of the Chicken.*)*

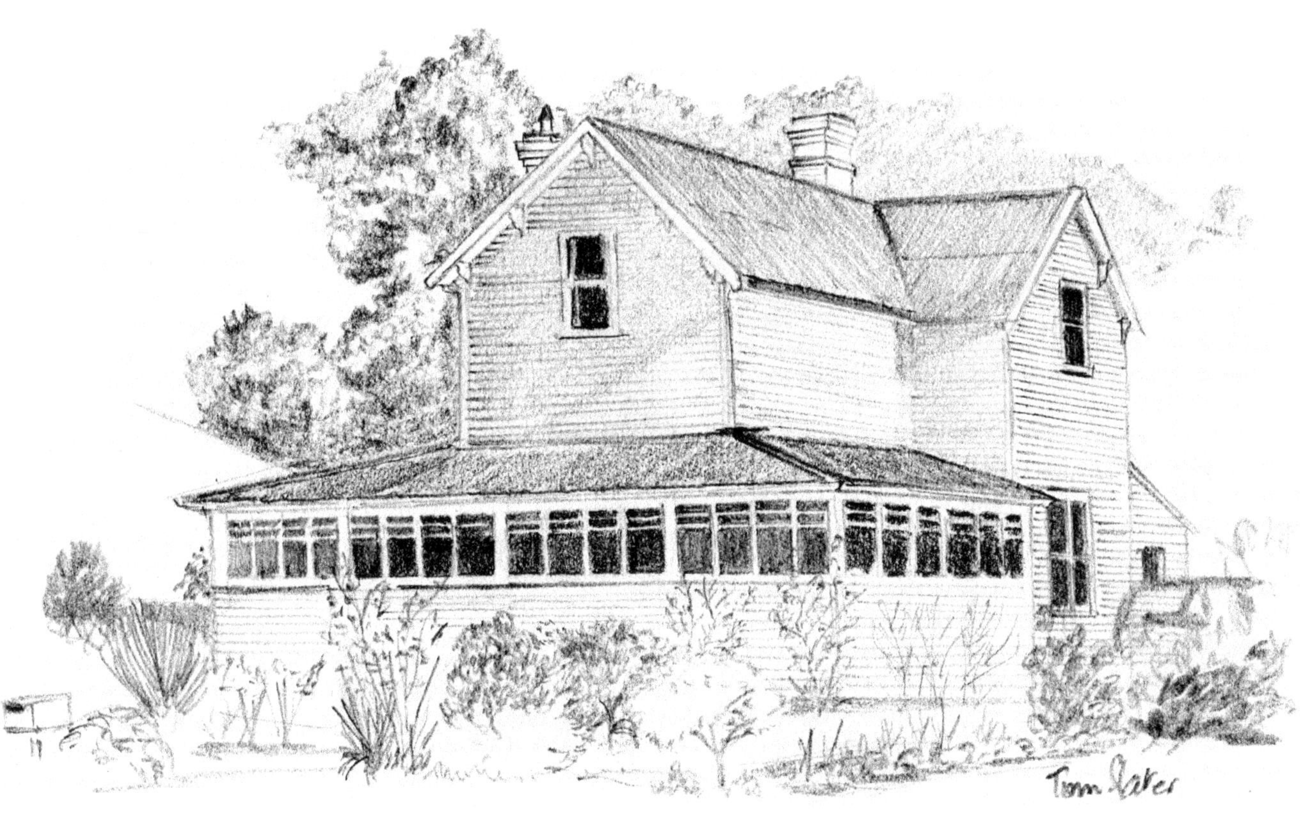

Woodland Health Retreat, Vic

Are you stressed out and in need of pampering? Has laying become a chore for you? Are uncomfortable perches creating issues in the back and legs? Or are you just feeling hen-pecked?

Woodland Retreat is owned and operated by Uneedit Health Farms, and is believed to be the first such farm in Australia dedicated exclusively to the health and welfare of the genus *Gallus Domesticus.* Even then there is a specific focus on layers in need of total rest and de-stressing. Here you will be waited on wing and foot, from dawn until dusk. Dependent chickens are also provided for in separate facilities away from the main therapy centre.

Its location in Central Victoria is very accessible. A bus service from the city drops you off at the farm gate. A pleasant stroll takes you to the buildings, set well back out of sight and sound of traffic.

A team of therapists is on wing at all times, but guests are free to simply have a wonderfully relaxing holiday. Medical certificates are not required.

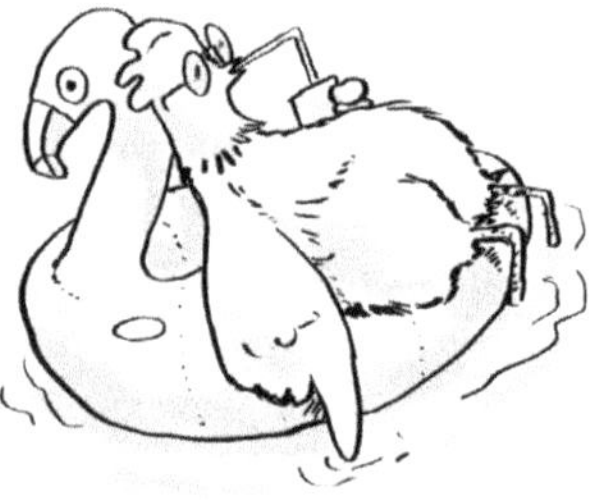

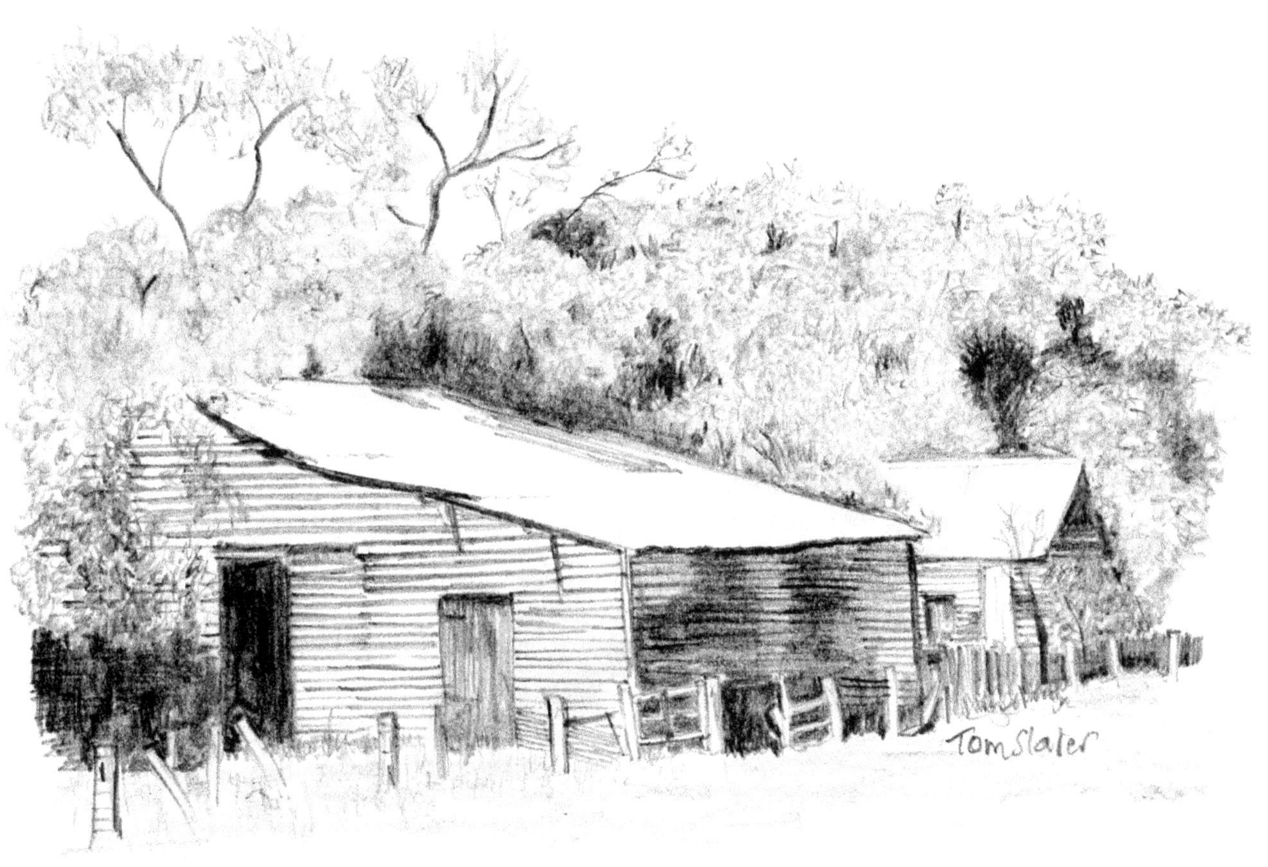
Tom Slater

Chotel Fingerboards, Vic

This attractive chook park takes its name from the multiple signposts close by, a landmark in this district in East Gippsland. The accommodation is top-class, and every improvement has been made by long exposure to the wind and rain, as well as by what humans would regard as general neglect. Missing weatherboards for easy access, and plenty of accumulated dirt, are just the beginning. A dilapidated tank stand provides an ideal playground for little chickens. Individual chickens and families are welcome, but larger groups may be provided for in the near future by the addition of a derelict schoolhouse from nearby Briagalong.

Proximity to the Fingerboards road junction means easy access to surrounding attractions, especially the Den of Nargun, which is not as spooky as it sounds but is a beautiful picnic spot on the Mitchell River. However guests must provide their own transport, which is usually no problem as that is the only way to get to Chotel Fingerboards in the first place.

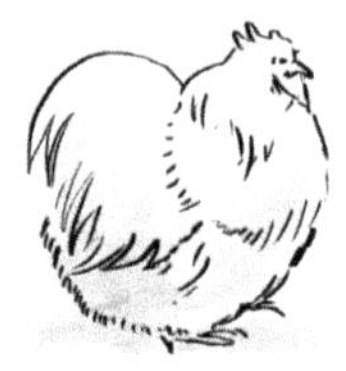

Brain teaser:
Which breed of chicken was named after the town of Orpington in England?

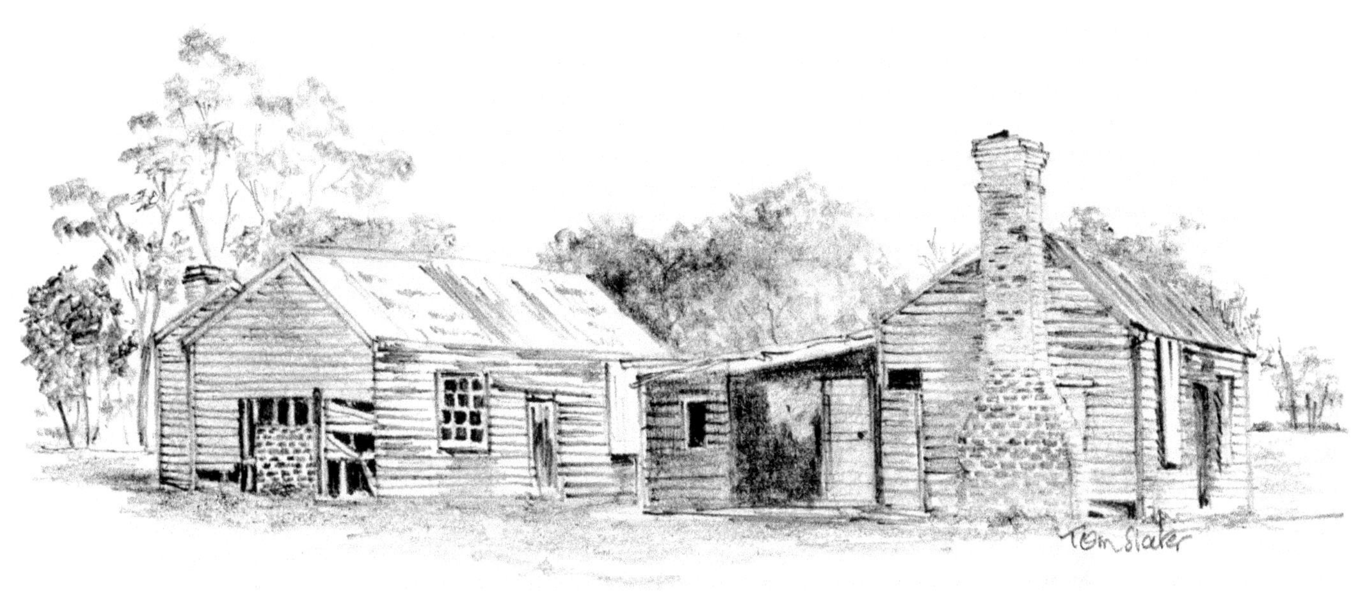

Mackay Harbour, Qld

Elizabeth E2 is one of the most unusual examples of poultry holiday accommodation in Australia.

Moored opposite the huge sugar terminal at Mackay, this vessel once took tours to the Barrier Reef, but was recently purchased by Laying Chooks Australia and fitted out as a floating chookotel. The vessel doubles as a floating headquarters for LCA, but the lower decks have been converted for accommodation. It boasts what are thought to be the only self-feeders in the world installed below the waterline of any operational maritime vessel of any kind of less than 20,000 tonnes.

Once a year, weather permitting, the vessel does a sightseeing tour down the coast to the massive Hay Point coal terminal, returning for a silo-door tasting at the sugar terminal wharf. An exclusive facility for the chook who has done everything, with a price to match.

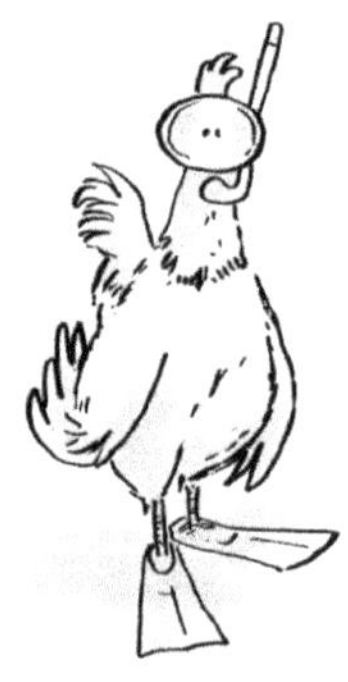

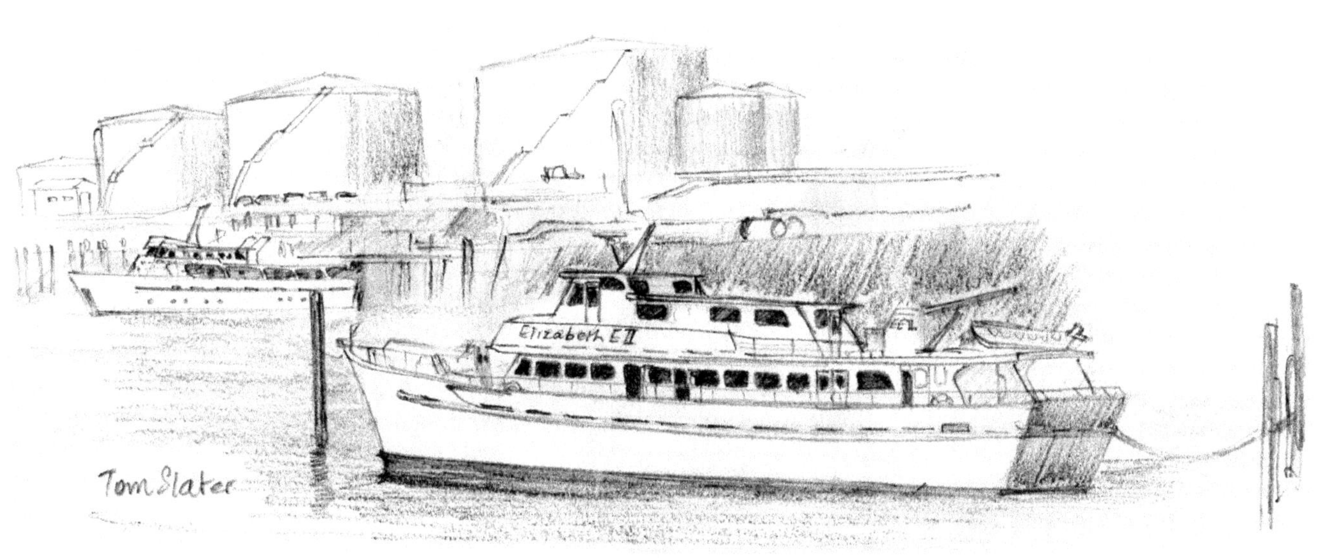
Elizabeth E II
Tom Slater

Miga Lake Chotel, Vic

This exceptionally attractive accommodation is a natural wonder, representing the triumph of storm and tempest over the human dwellings that have marred the landscape of Western Victoria for over 200 years. While not quite 'back to nature', this chotel offers the best in rough and rugged chook accommodation. You can't fail to enjoy the variety of perching places on remnant furniture, the accumulated dust, and other internal facilities such as the old bathroom mirror.

Recreational opportunities abound in the immediate area. Set the kids to play hide-and-seek under the fallen verandah, which also provides access for the sure-footed to the roof for distant views of Miga Lake and beyond. Specially designed three-pronged water skis may be hired locally by would-be skiers, but check that there is water in the lake first as it is disappointing to make the trip and have to resort to the same old scratch and preen to pass the time.

This location is a great side-trip if you take the long cut while you are travelling from Sydney to Adelaide via Balranald and Swan Hill. Turn left at Swan Hill and proceed via Sea Lake, Hopetoun, Rainbow, Jeparit, and Nhill, to mention just the main places, before turning directly south for 70 kms. You can then resume the trip to Adelaide via Edenhope, Naracoorte, Bordertown and all points west.

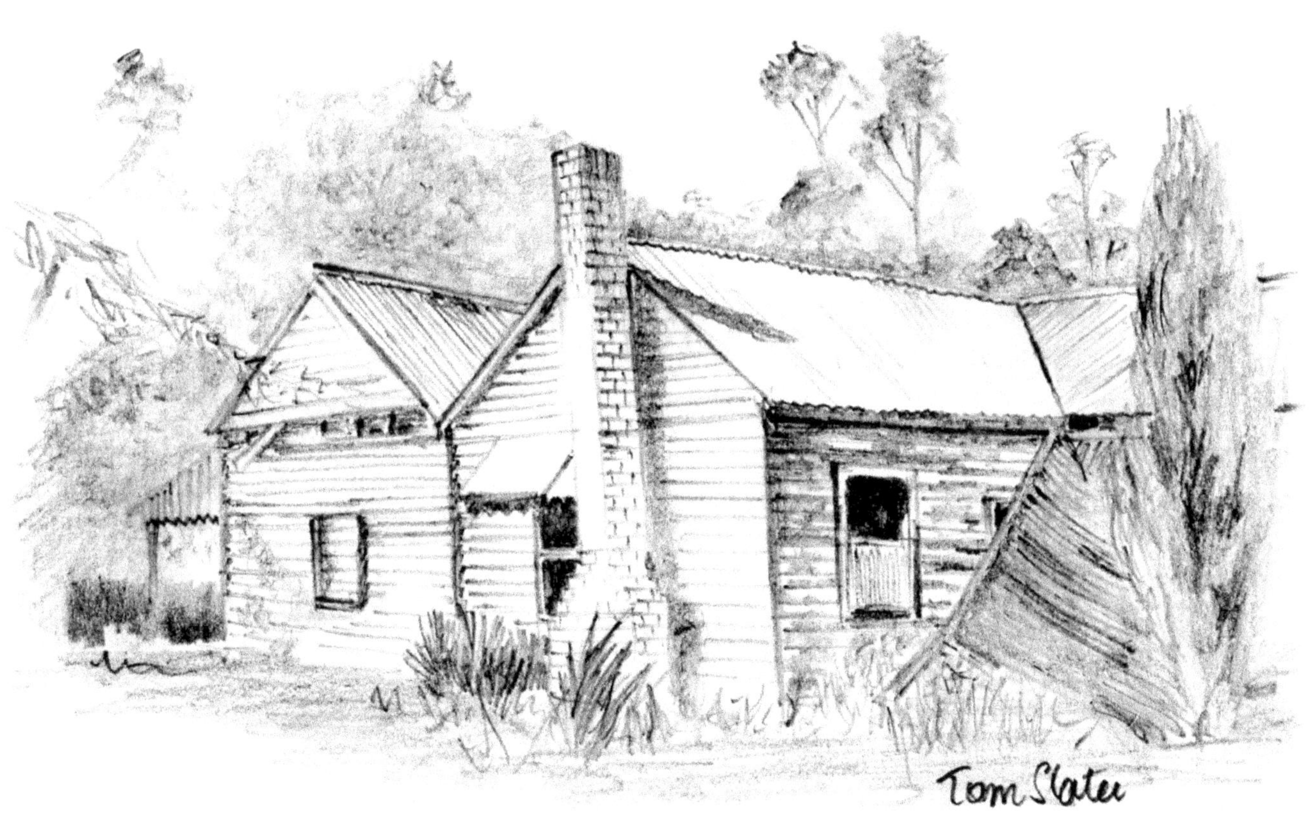
Tom Slater

Chotel Silverton, NSW

Silverton is an old mining town which once had a population of 500, but now has around 40 residents. Its existence was due to silver mining, and a number of historic buildings remain. Tours of the old silver mine are one of the attractions, but it is the wide open spaces and rugged frontier feel of the place that attracts tourists, both human and bird.

Every four years, to coincide with the Olympic Games, Silverton runs a competition to find the person or chook who comes nearest to pronouncing correctly the word Umberumberka, the name of the local reservoir and the creek on which the town is situated. This is an internationally unique competition, not least because chooks and other birds have as much chance of winning as humans. Open only to visitors, so you will be in with a chance.

Accommodation for poultry is offered at the Chotel Silverton, pictured.

If you have been to Silverton in Colorado, USA, you may know that it is a Statutory Town that is the county seat of, and the only incorporated municipality in, San Juan County. It is a waste of time looking for any resemblance to Silverton in NSW. It is rumoured that an astronaut once saw both Silvertons at the same time, but this is probably impossible even for an astronaut.

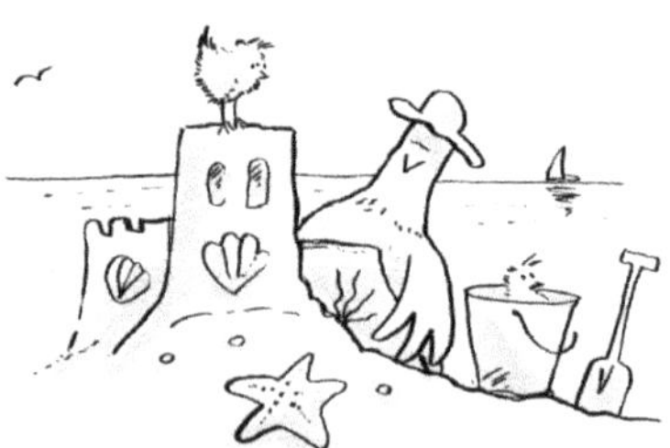

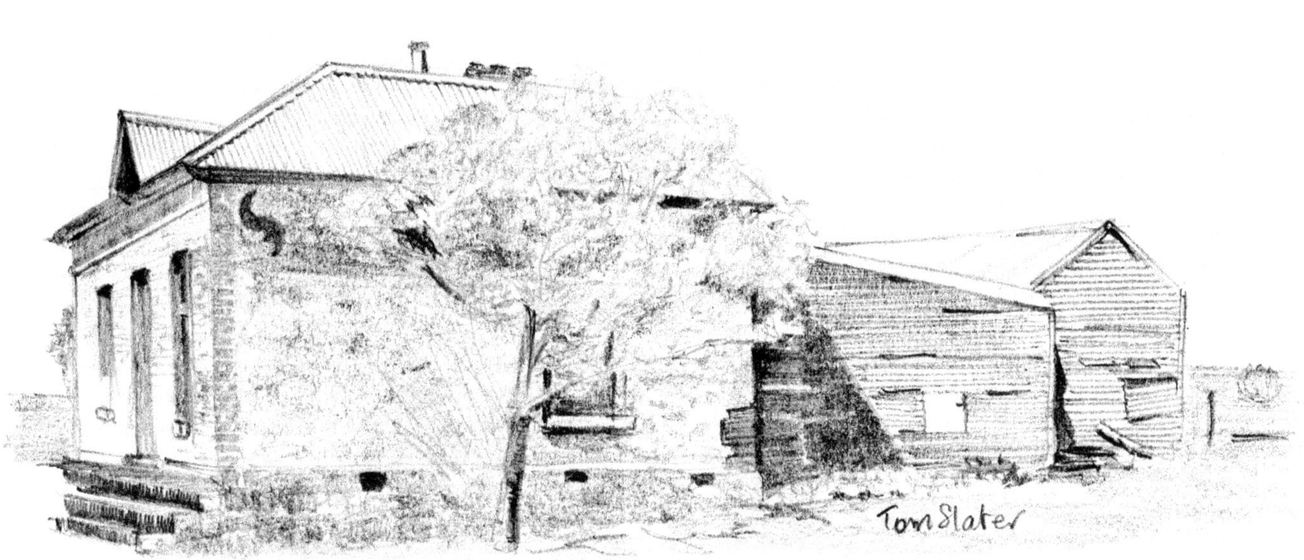
Tom Slater

The Railway Siding, Central Vic

The decrepit platform, office and sheds at this disused railway siding are an example of how to have a holiday on a shoe-string budget. No longer operated by the Victorian Railways, bookings are made through the local shire. A regional bus service will pick you up from the post office, provided that you are securely enclosed in a cardboard box, wire cage or similar. Scattered barley, oats and wheat are still to be found in the big shed, so food supplies are assured. No keys required, but you are asked to let Mrs Hennington across the road know when you arrive, in case of emergency.

If anyone knows exactly where this old platform and shed are, please contact the publishers so that details can be included in subsequent editions.

Unfortunately the author failed to note where this siding was when he did a quick sketch while his wife put down a rebellion in the back seat. He admits to being quite impressed by his own ability to remember all the details above, having only had a quick read of the faded poster that was nailed to the side of the shed.

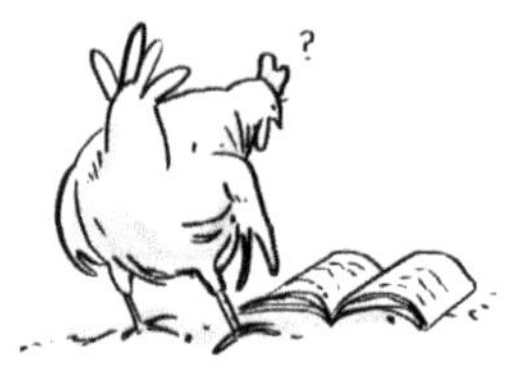

One thesaurus gives 'paltry' as a synonym for chickenfeed. Fancy a thesaurus, of all things, not being able to spell 'poultry'.

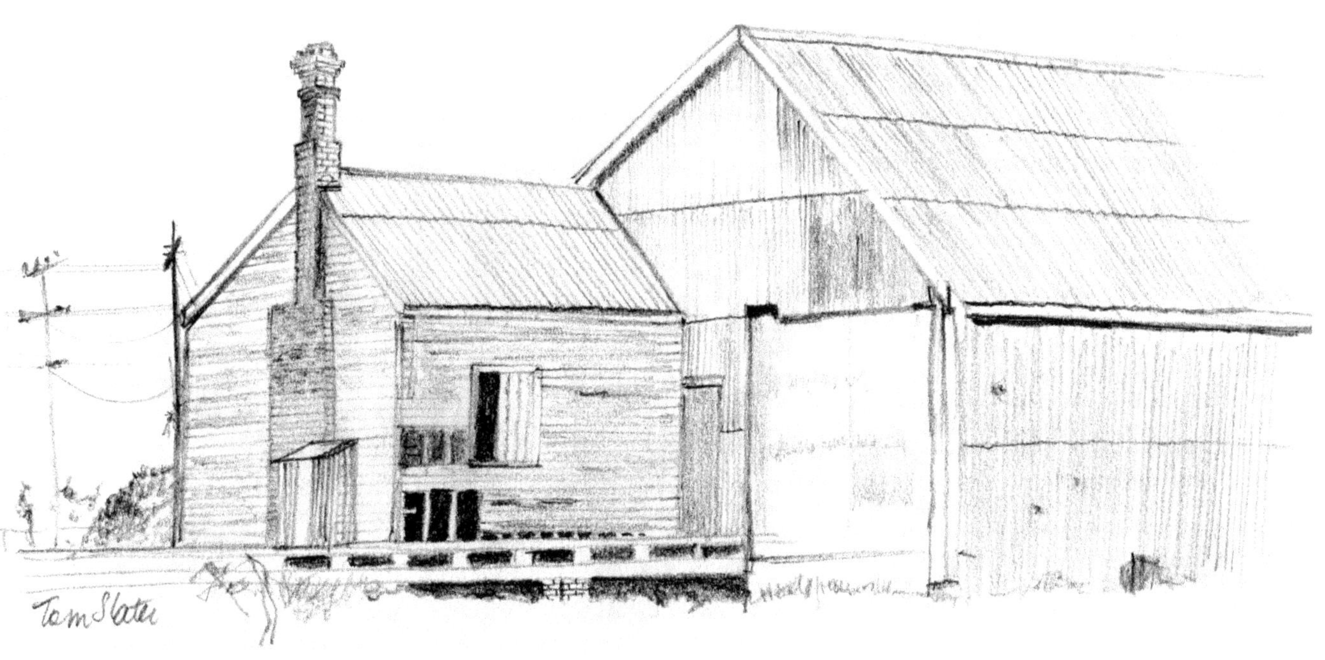
Tom Slater

Yangery Grange Homestead

Yangery Grange homestead was built around 1895. Dramatically refurbished in the 21st century, this is luxury accommodation at its finest – humanly speaking. But despite this it is still a welcome place for holidaying hens. There are just five exclusive units among the homestead buildings, each with its own feeding arrangements and exceptionally comfortable perches. For conferences, guest speakers and dignitaries can be accommodated here while the bulk of participants can be domiciled in the numerous outbuildings (see Yangery Grange entry in part two).

The district of Yangery is adjacent to the district of Yarpturk in Western Victoria. Someone has worked out that of the 188 places within 100kms of Yarpturk, Yangery is the nearest. Yarpturk itself is said to be exactly 870.75 kms from Wollongong. This will be of interest to chooks planning to fly in from Wollongong, as the Warrnambool airport is just a stone's throw from Yangery Grange, and for the return trip, Yangery Grange is just a stone's throw from Warrnambool airport.

A goose is not a chicken. But if I said a particular goose was chicken (not a chicken, just chicken) it would mean something different, and could arguably be true.

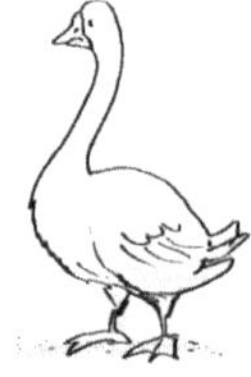

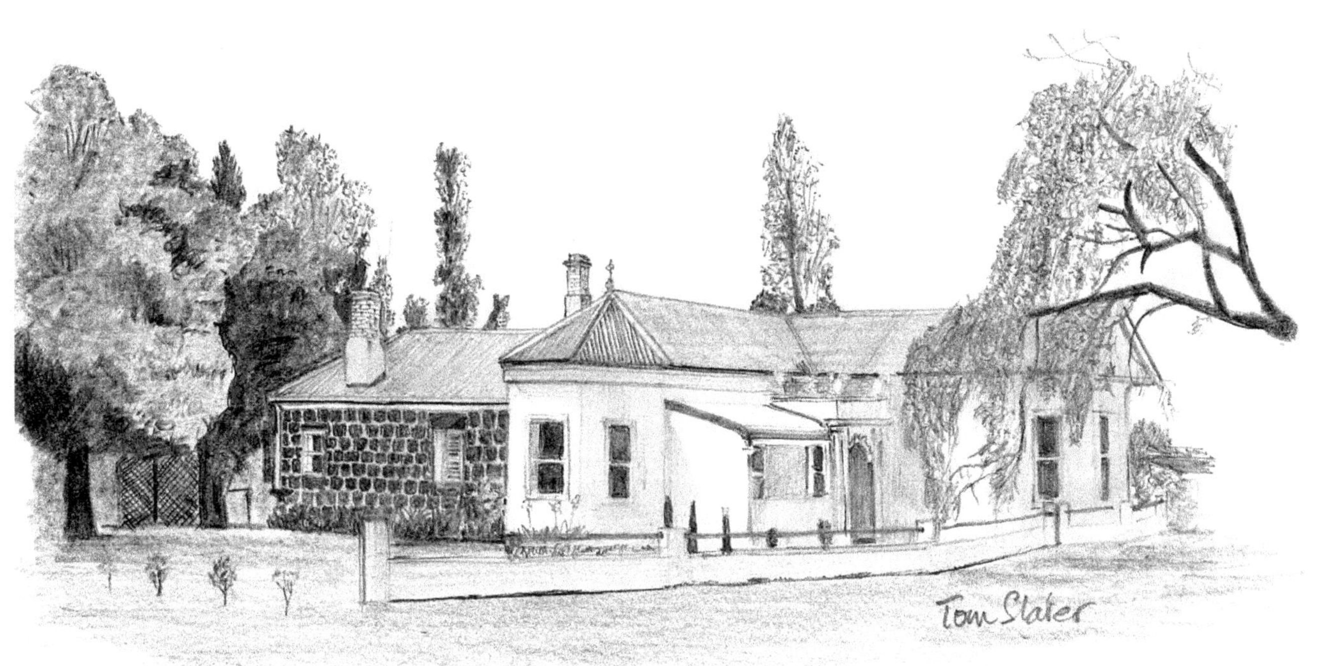
Tom Slater

The Camp, NT

Ranking amongst the most unusual chook holiday destinations, The Camp offers chooks the opportunity to experience a holiday in a variety of essentially human situations – old style caravans, pop-up vans, derelict vehicles, and most popular, in wurlies made from local bush.

A permit to camp here is required as the access road passes through Aboriginal lands and communities.

Donkeys, wild horses and camels roam freely, and the local ranger offers lectures on the destructive impact of these introduced animals on the land and vegetation, and how chooks can avoid the pitfalls of free ranging.

This is a holiday with a purpose, equipping chooks with knowledge and skills for ecologically sustainable foraging when they return home.

This is one place where the chook owner should accompany his flock. Even a week in an Aboriginal community can clear away many of the prejudices and ignorance that is the lot of many 'introduced' Australians. The deprivations suffered as a result of the white invasion are all too evident, but so too is the intelligence, dignity, determination and achievement of a people who, having survived all the odds, live there, and who maintain what they can of a traditional culture which shows up some of the deficiencies of our own individualistic and materialistic western way of life.

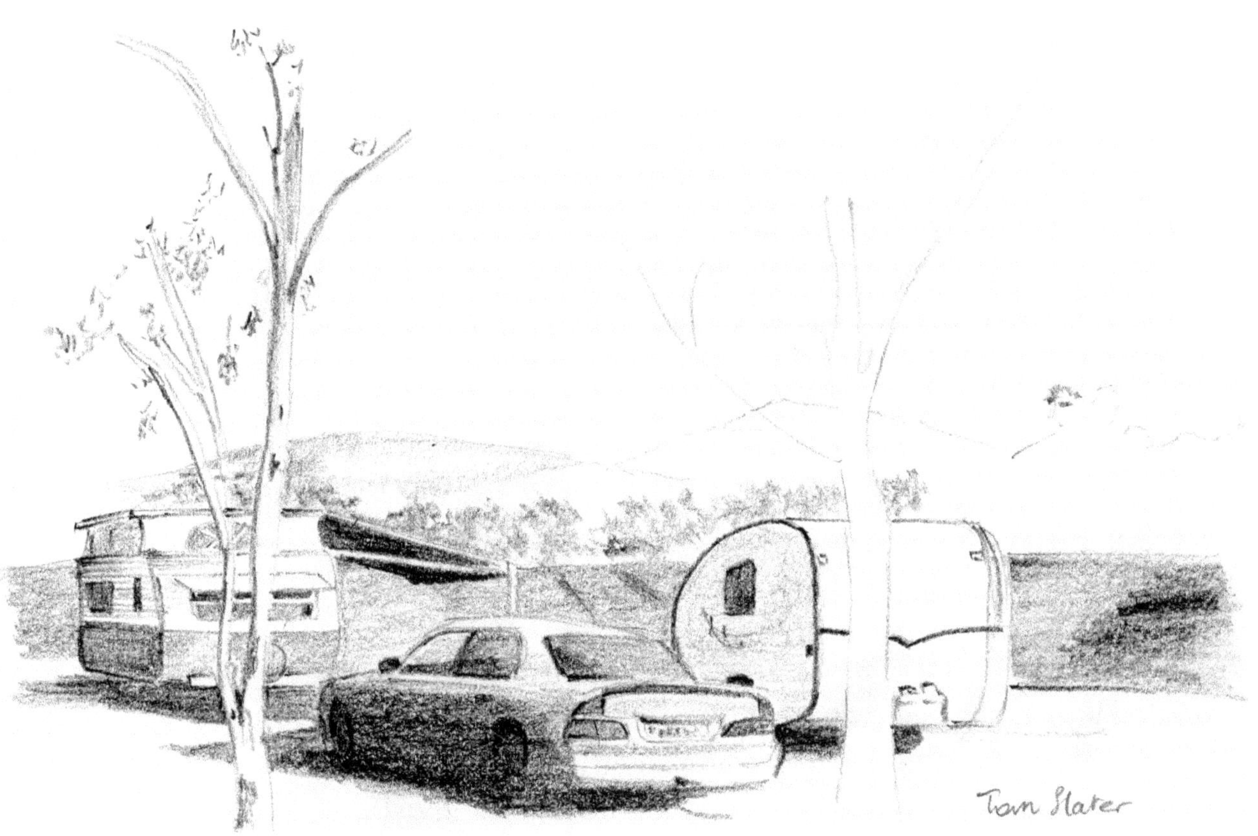
Tom Slater

Machinery Shed, Glenlee, Vic

This beautifully unrestored machinery shed is another holiday destination for the agriculturally minded chook.

Sleeping options include under-canvas (old vehicle thrown in), straight dirt floor, standard perches of all sizes, rafters for the aeronautically inclined, and assorted pieces of old machinery. Even newer machinery, such as the grain augers, can be utilised by small chickens, one per auger.

Nearby attractions include Lake Hindmarsh, which, being often dry, is well-suited to non-swimmers, and the town of Jeparit, birthplace of Sir Robert Menzies. Although not particularly known as a poultry person, it is of interest to know that Menzies was Prime Minister (read Chief Chook) of Australia for many years.

It so happens that this shed is on a farm formerly owned by the flying bush padre Don Kube, and now operated by Andrew, one of his sons, alongside his own aviation business. Don was a larger than life character with a passion for aviation and for sharing his faith. He was famously featured in the 'Day in the Life of Australia' in 1981, where he was pictured presiding over a lonely bush funeral in the far north west of Western Australia.

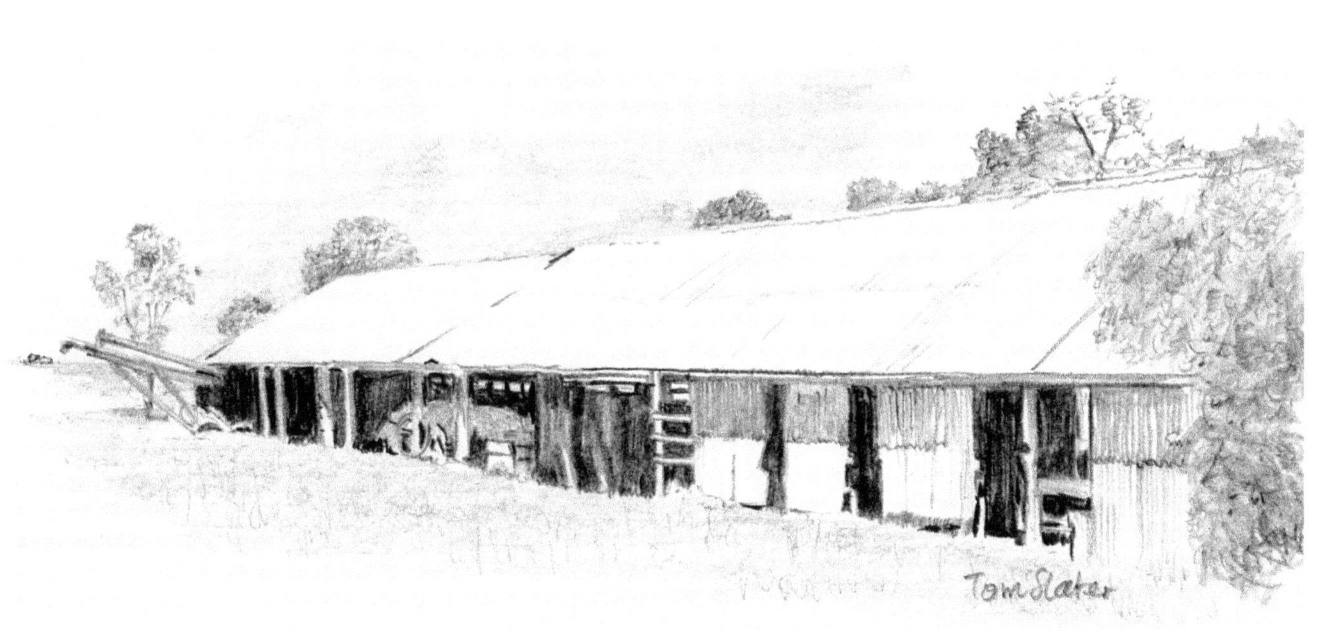
Tom Slater

St Francis Retreat, SA

Named after the famous patron saint of animals, including birds, the St Francis of Assissi Wellbeing retreat is thought to be the only Retreat in Australia, indeed the southern hemisphere, for chickens seeking to master mindfulness.

It is operated by Trappist monks who practice the vow of silence, so peace is pretty much guaranteed for the chook seeking an extended period of quiet contemplation.

Situated in the lower Flinders Ranges in South Australia, the retreat offers unsurpassed solitude. A local friar bird is available for counselling and support, especially for those choosing to fast (a good option in this situation, except when the crops are ripening in the summer when temptation is most severe.)

Maximum of one guest at any one time, for obvious reasons. Discount available for chickens with a medical certificate.

In order to preserve the tranquillity and privacy of the retreat, its precise location is not made known until the chook's deposit has been left. Let me re-phrase that – until the chook has made the necessary monetary down-payment. The author considers himself fortunate to have discovered it by accident, and has since sent one of his more unsettled chickens to the Retreat for a week that changed its life.

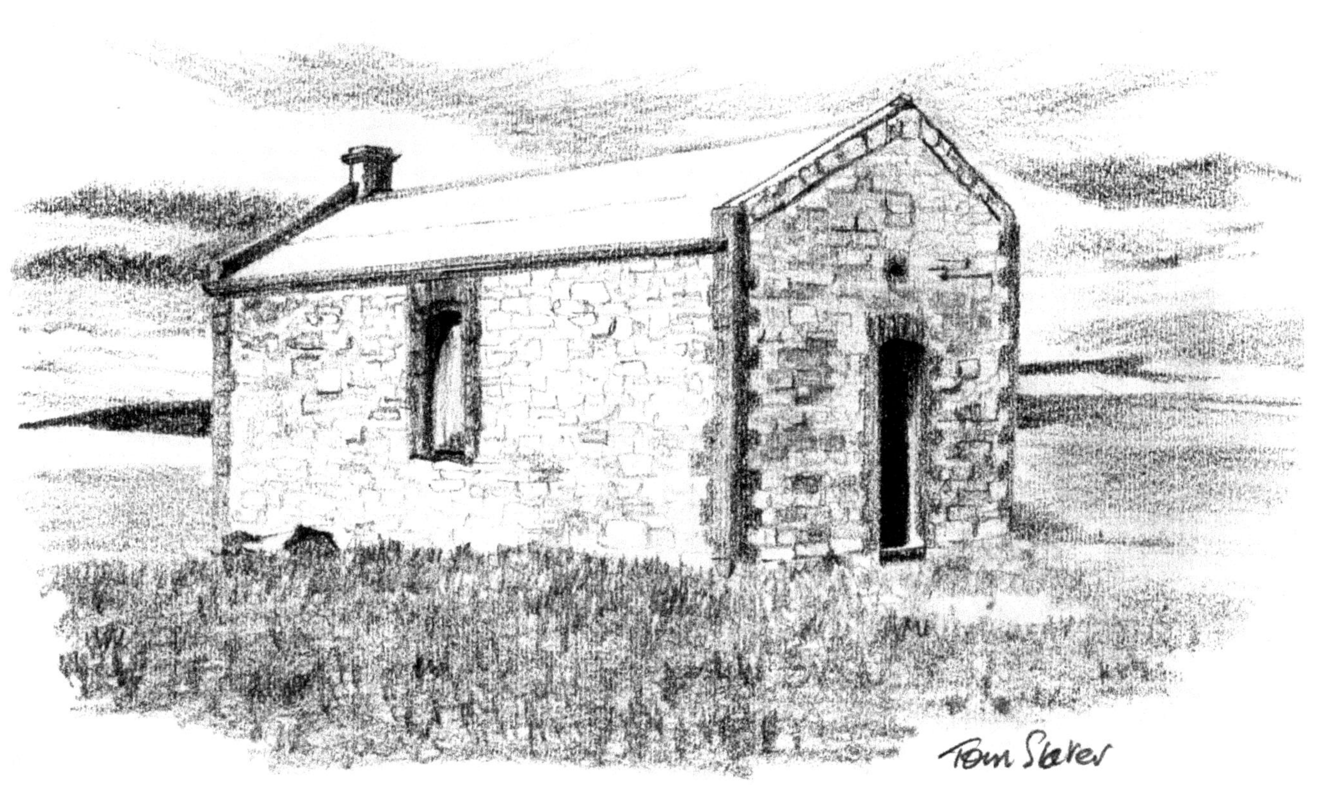
Tom Slater

Feathers of Fingal, Tas

The town of Fingal is in the beautiful Fingal Valley in northern Tasmania, just 15 minutes from St Mary's (though if you are walking, strutting or scratching around *en route*, a lot longer). At the rear of a historic emporium in Fingal is the exclusive Feathers of Fingal B&B. The old stone building has everything the holidaying hen could ask for – security, but with easy access; a loft with views, old tractor tyres, a chimney, choices of décor – both corrugated iron and stonework – and the unmistakeable ambience of a place no longer inhabited by humans.

A major attraction of Fingal is the view of the Ben Lomond Plateau to the north, and especially the spectacular Stacks Bluff, which can be viewed by any reasonably agile chook from the roof of the old post office, which can be accessed via a tall tree at the eastern end.

Feathers of Fingal opened as a Chicken B&B in 1953 but shot to prominence two years later when the first proprietor was elected to the Tasmanian Parliament, the first (and so far the only) chook ever to have that honour. 'Feathers', as it is known to locals, was awarded B&B of the year in 2019 by the Fingal Valley Tourist Association, beating two other contestants.

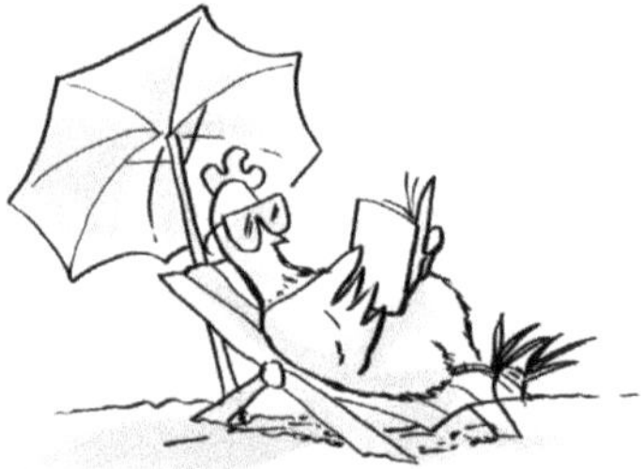

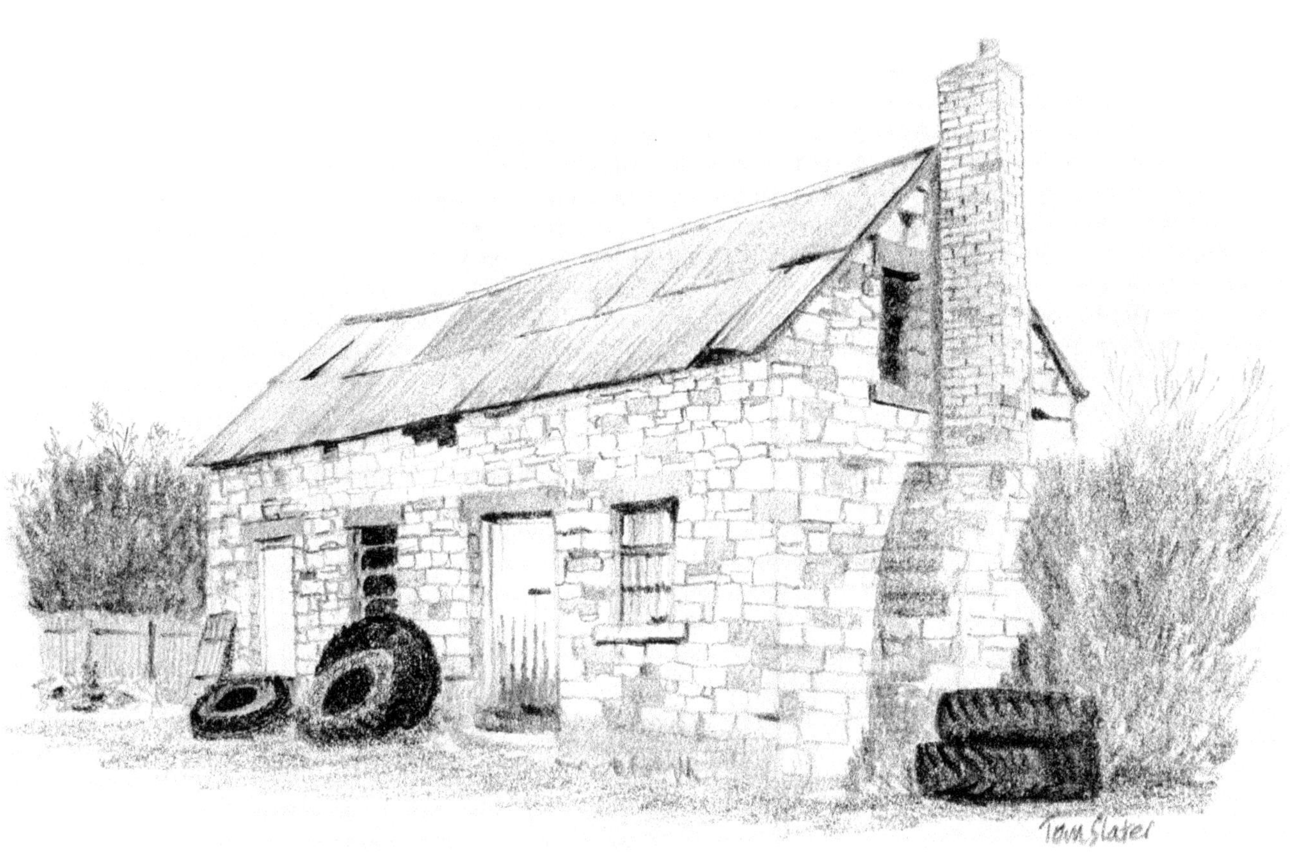
Tom Slater

Charters Towers, Qld

Charters Towers was the first town in Australia to be declared a Chook-friendly Town. The award recognises the almost unlimited variety of accommodation within the boundaries of the town, which has something of a Wild West feel about its main street. It certainly is west (of Townsville), but also east (of Hughenden, Richmond, Julia Creek, Cloncurry and Mount Isa in that order, plus places in-between. More east than west, you might say. Still it is west of Fiji and the Cook Islands, Chile, Bolivia and Brazil, which is a lot of being west of.

One of the tourist attractions of CT is Ghost Tours, but they are not for the chicken-hearted, so it is pointless mentioning them. Forget it. There are numerous natural wonders to be explored, and a wealth of activities for tourists, though many chickens prefer shopping in the town's emporiums to trekking along the extensive walking paths around the town and district so favoured by humans.

On average it only rains on one day in September in Charters Towers, which will be of particular interest to chickens who may be allergic to heavy rain. The average overnight temperature in December is 22 degrees, and with more rain around the atmosphere at that time may be what meteorologists refer to as 'muggy'. It is advisable to take a fan at this time of the year.

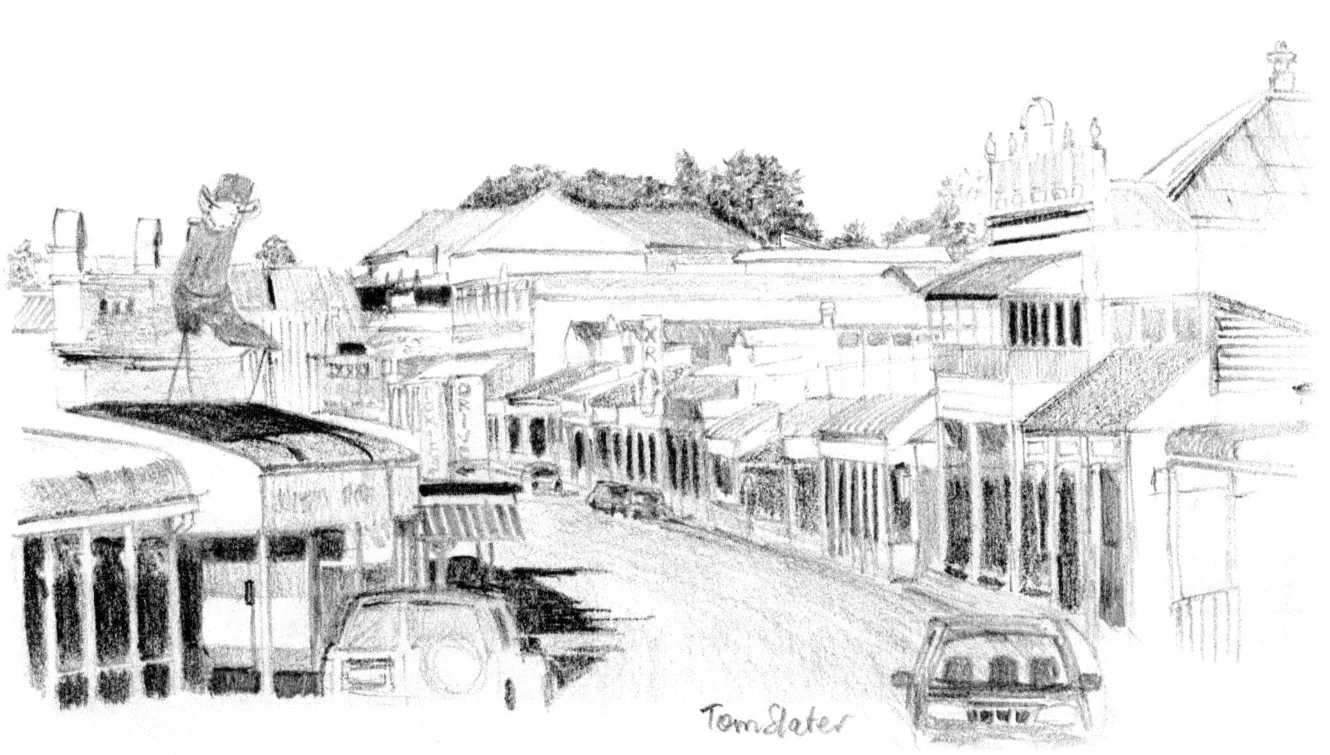
Tom Slater

Ross Cottage, Tas

Situated just off the Midland Highway, the historic town of Ross is blindingly beautiful, if that's not some sort of contradiction in terms. At least bits of it are, like the famous bridge, a superb example of architecture and of the skills of the convicts who built it, and so many other bridges and buildings in Tasmania. It also has perhaps the world's ugliest hair-dressing salon, but that in itself is an attraction of sorts. How many places can boast any building of that unique distinction? Other attractions include the remains of the old Female Factory (a former workhouse for female convicts) and several lovely stone churches.

Ross Cottage stands somewhere between the bridge and the hairdressing salon – architecturally speaking, that is. However the salient point for the hen seeking a good holiday is that it has a very nice chicken coop in the garden, and a very nice chap who comes each day to check on guests and re-supply the feed and water containers.

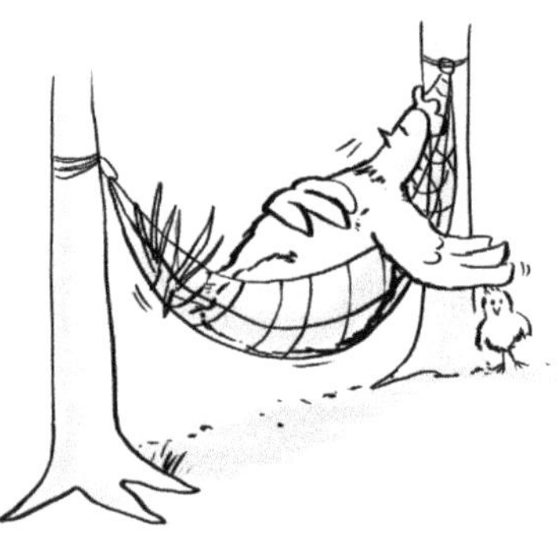

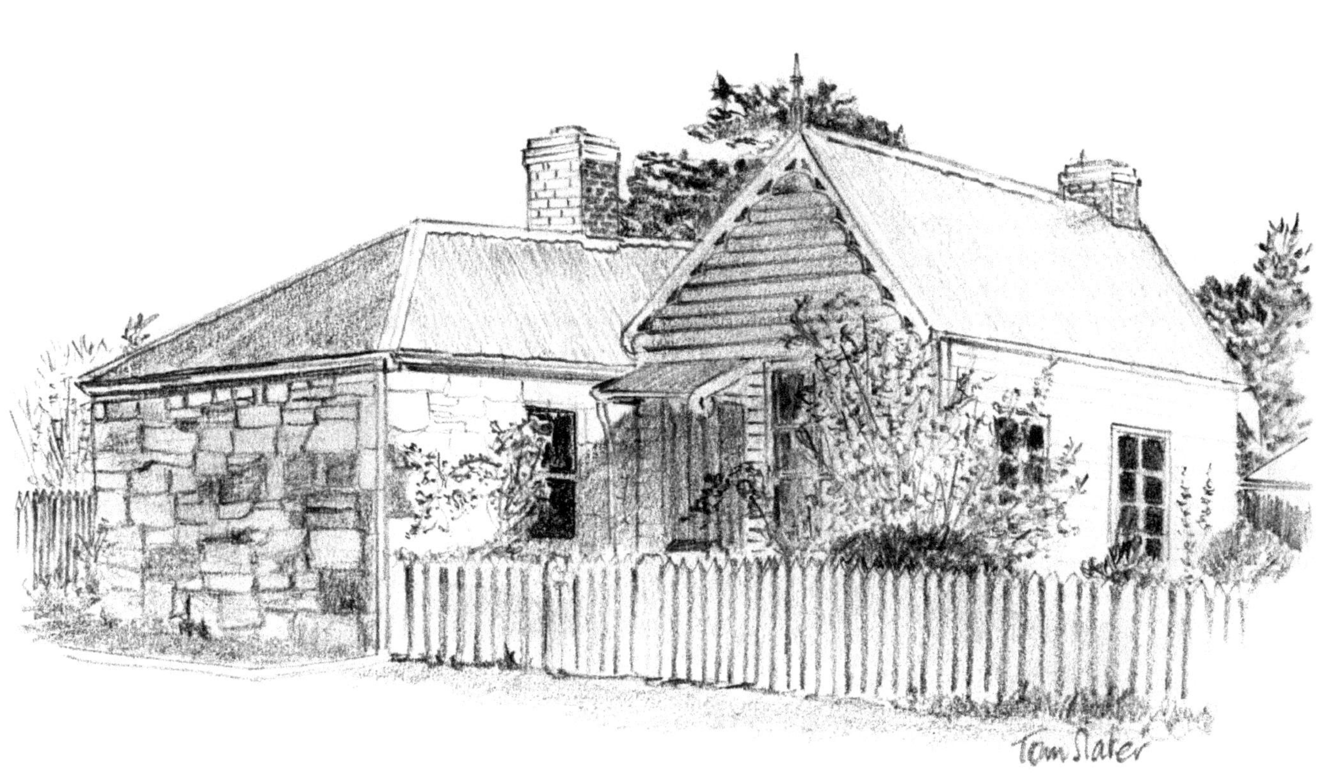
Tom Slater

The Inn, Malmsbury, Vic

Few chook holiday destinations bring to mind so readily a pivotal moment of history – in this case, around 4BC when there was 'no room in the inn' for Mary and Joseph, and they had to stay in some sort of animal shelter.

The Inn at Malmsbury uses this historical motif in the naming of its various chook units, all located in the sheds at the back of The Inn, a bluestone mansion. Names like the Bethlehem Suite, The Magi Room, Cows Corner and The Guiding Star Restaurant evoke the Biblical story.

Chooks of all religions are welcome to the annual service celebrating the grain harvest, held in the garden shed, and attracting poultry from all over Victoria. Unlimited free-ranging in the surrounding paddocks.

'CHICKENS is a (sic) 8 letter word starting with C and ending with S.'
(source: www.the-crossword-solver.com)

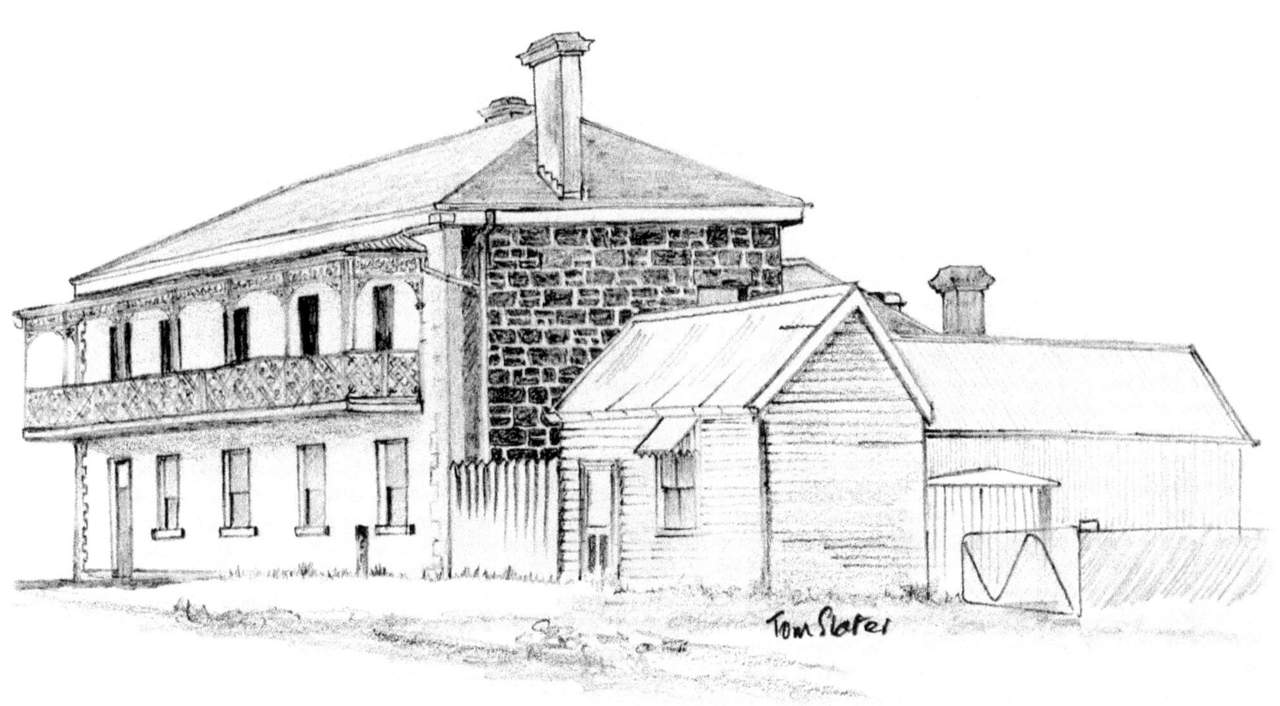
Tom Slater

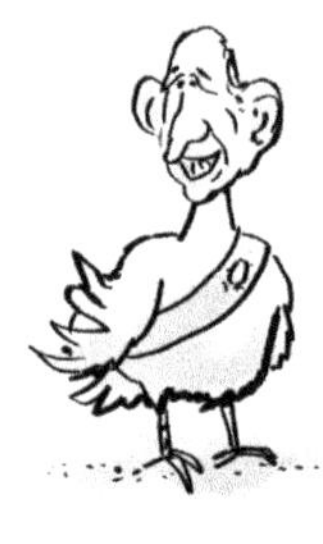

Famous people who like chickens include Theodore Roosevelt, who kept a number of chickens at the White House, including a pet one-legged rooster. Prince Charles and Oprah Winfrey both keep chickens. Also Reese Witherspoon, and Tori Spelling, whoever she is.

PART TWO

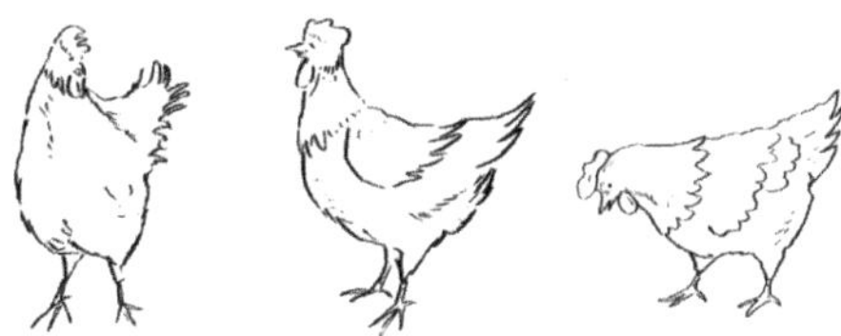

Accommodation for large groups and conferences

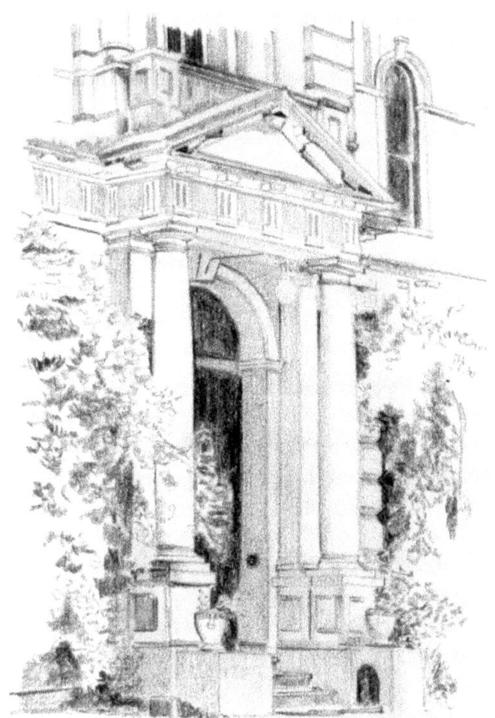

Entrance to Noorilim homestead near Nagambie, Victoria.

The Silos, Charlton, Vic

It is obvious why The Silos at Charlton has become one of the most popular conference centres for the Australian poultry sector. Dominating the town as you approach it from any direction, The Silos was voted Feathers Magazine's Conference Centre of the Year every year from 2012 to 2013. It also contains the highest poultry penthouse in the southern hemisphere. The International President of Chickenry (a Rhode Island Red from South Africa) and the King of Botswana both stayed here in 2013 during the triennial International Chicken Forum, which was held in Charlton two years in a row.

Naturally the best views are not available to chooks housed in other parts of the vast complex, but Tourism Charlton recommends a drive to Mount Dooboobetic (no kidding) which is off Back Teddywaddy Road (seriously) for panoramic views of the town and countryside.

For the gourmet hen, the award-winning Gate 5 Restaurant features a great variety of locally grown wheat, barley and other grains, raw or cooked.

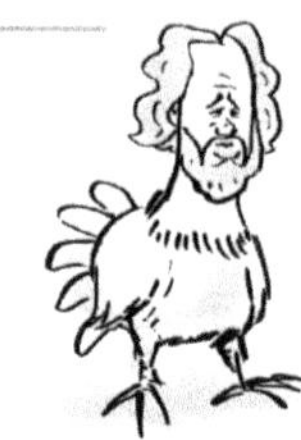

According to a list of popular chicken names on happychickencoop.com's website, 'Gregory Peck' and 'Russell Crowe' are popular names for chickens. But since this book is about hen health we may be excused for mentioning only 'Meryl Cheep' and 'Yolko Ono'.

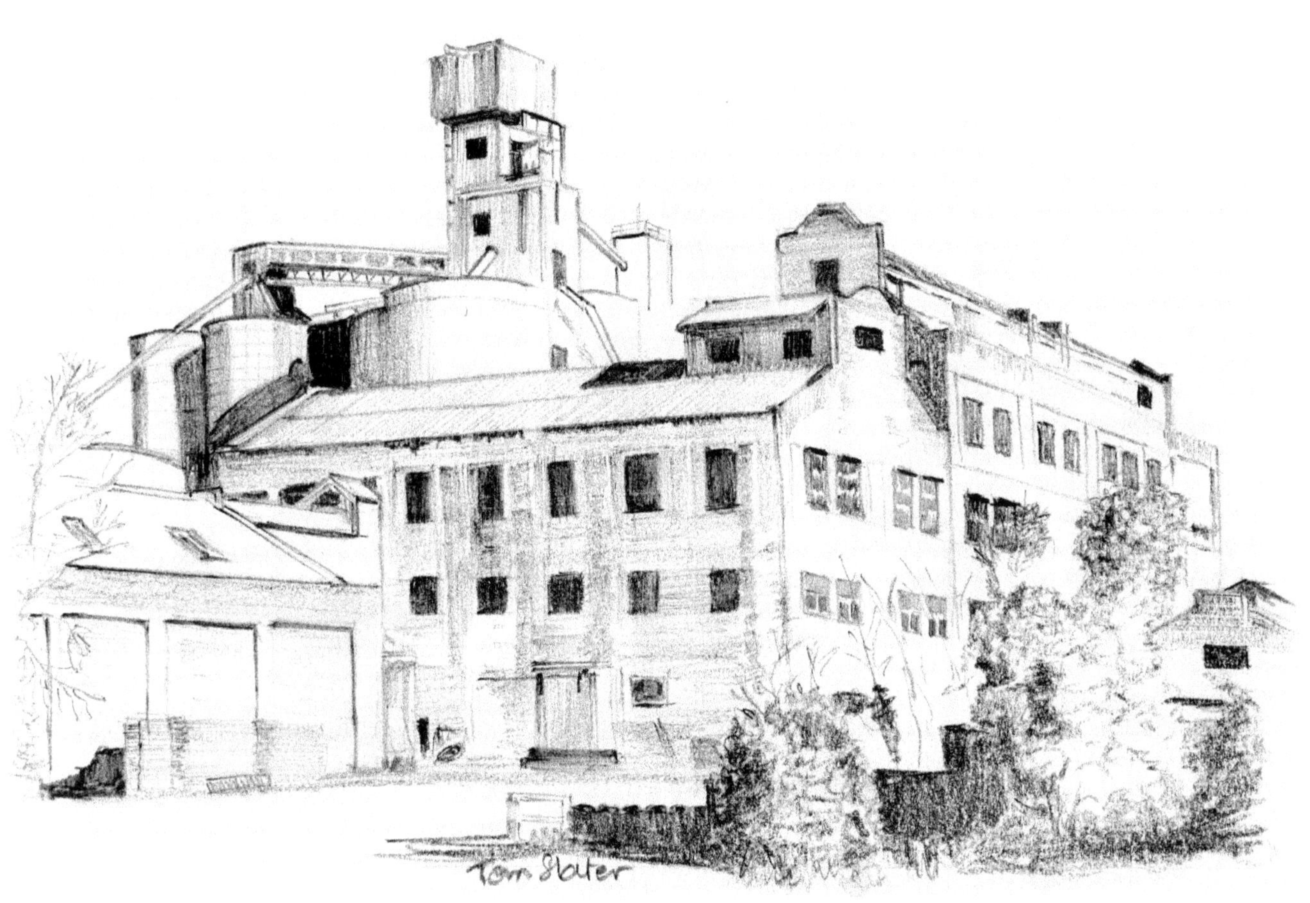
Tom Slater

Browns Plaster Works, Shepparton, Vic

One of Australia's premier chook resorts, the plaster works offers an endless variety of units for the chook holiday. From ground level apartments to the best galvanised iron condominiums high in the roof spaces, there is so much to explore you'll never have to leave the resort.

Hungry? Check out the nearby banks of the Goulburn River for a wide variety of the local slugs and insects.

Every evening, except for Monday to Wednesday, weekends and public holidays, the Maître d' of Chicken Accommodation hosts a Happy Hour (BYO drinks) in the main moulding room, and delivers a lecture on the history of plaster, before reciting her own poetry, which focuses (possibly uniquely) on the trials, tribulations and joys of plaster manufacture.

Browns Plaster works is a leading player in the Australian walls and ceilings industry, an industry you hadn't ever thought about I bet. This premises was originally the home of the Shepparton Soap Works, back in the late 19th century. The Brown family have been in plaster since 1927. Unimaginable. I was in plaster myself once with a broken arm, and I was sick of it in two weeks.

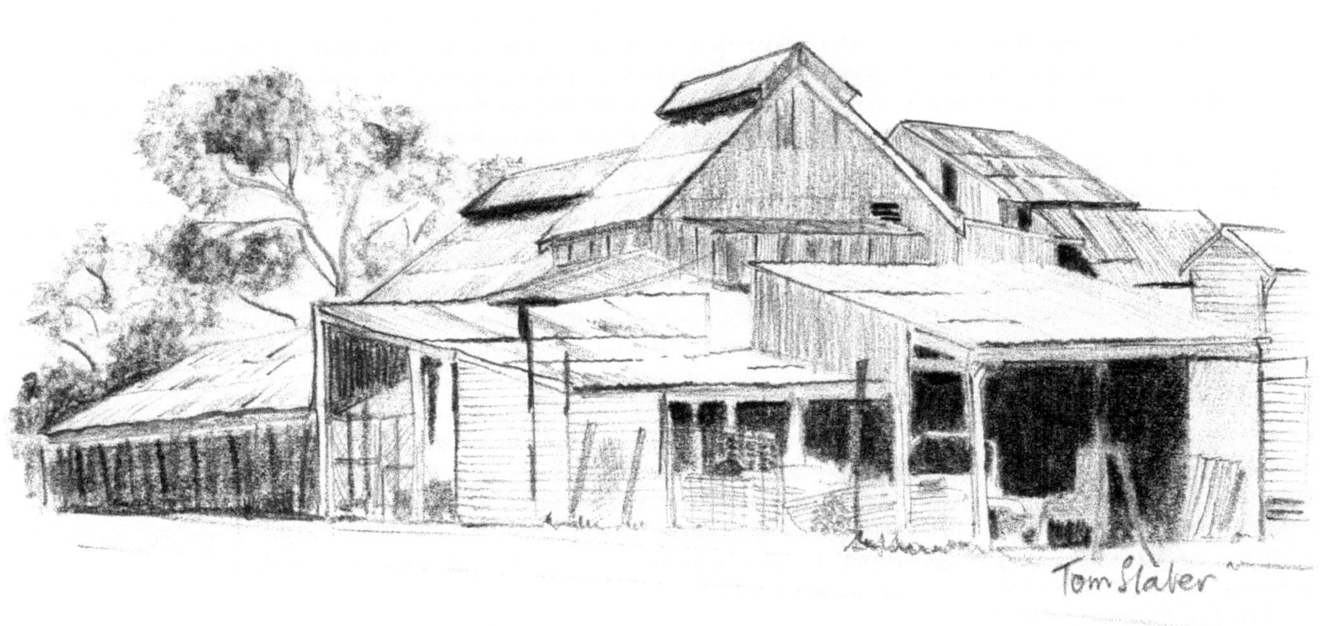
Tom Slater

Kinchega Woolshed, NSW

This magnificent shearing shed on the former Kinchega Station dates from 1875. Kinchega is now a national park.

Despite its relative remoteness, over 100 kms south of Broken Hill and 200 kms west of Ivanhoe, the Kinchega woolshed has attracted hens from all over Australia, especially for the annual conferences of the Country Chickens' Association.

The shed itself is enormous, and features a steam traction engine that first powered the machinery stands.

Close to the Darling River, the shed can be accessed by canoe several times each century during floods, but even the fittest chooks take months for the journey, and given the unpredictability of river flows, no chook has yet managed to arrive at the annual conference before closing day. The road trip from Ivanhoe is a beak-jarring experience on corrugations, and few survive it without mental scars. Be a brain, go by train to Broken Hill and hitch-hike. Several cars a day travel the road to nearby Menindee, and the local animal shelter provides a shuttle bus into the Park.

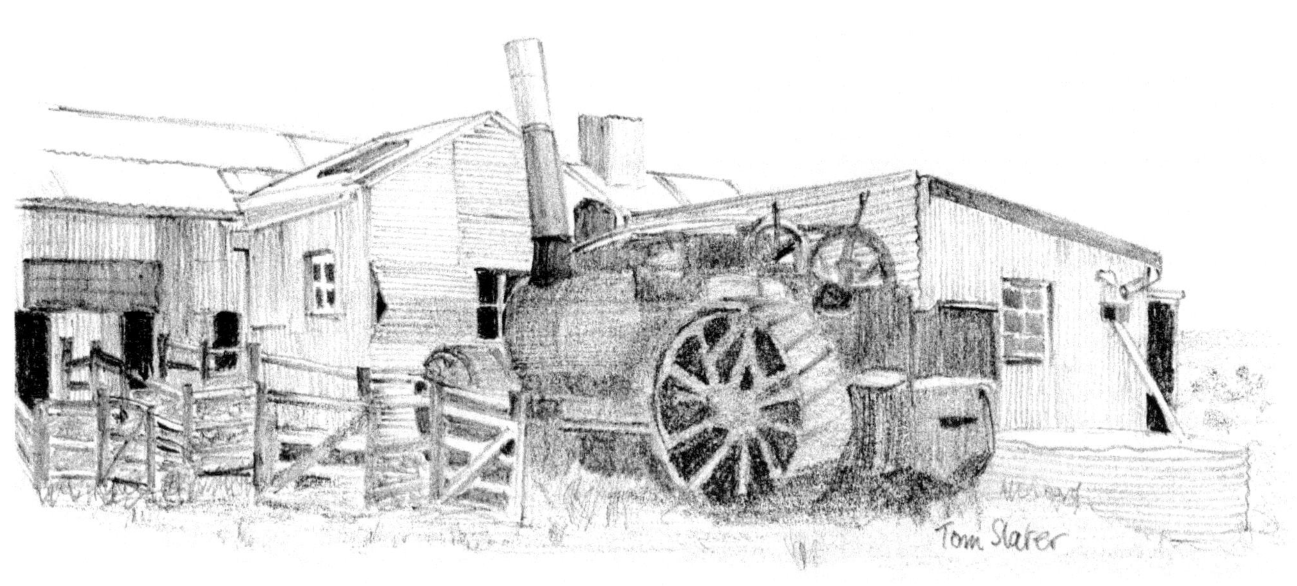
Tom Slater

Wonnerup Resort, WA

This magnificent historic resort is owned and operated by The Royal Chicken Society of WA, under licence from the National Trust.

Accommodation options range from luxury units in galvanised iron, to stone buildings more suitable to the budget-conscious hen.

The Wonnerup Experience offers the chance to pretend you are a human 100 years ago, and sleep in a four-poster bed and use a chamber pot at night.

Security is assured with a team of Alpacas on duty night and day.

Day trips include a number of scenic paddocks, the old windmill, the old homestead, the old tankstand and a whole lot of other old buildings and things. Of particular interest is a memorial obelisk located near the front gate, erected in honour of Edwina of Wonnerup, the only hen in Australia to lay 360 eggs in a calendar year. Open to RCSWA members and non-members alike.

Of course the modern chook is not always interested in human history, but that will not detract from the chook experience here at Wonnerup, where the particular needs of poultry are well understood and catered for. For example meals are served on the ground outside the back door rather than in the dining room, and there is no insistence on using the WCs and other facilities, provided that those activities are kept away from the immediate vicinity of the house.

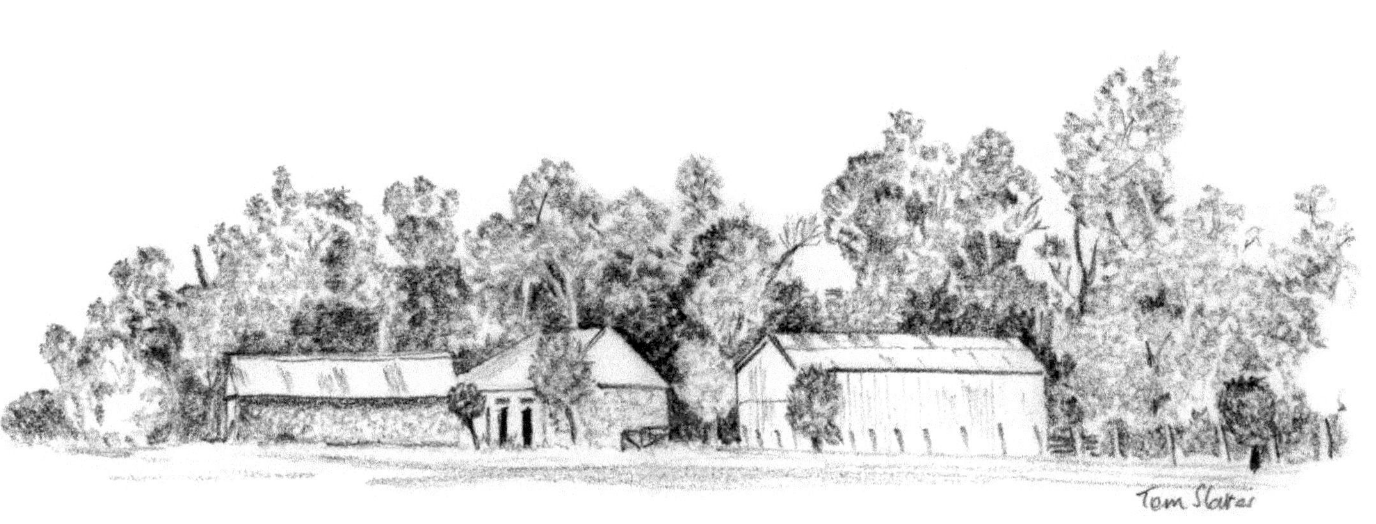
Tom Slater

The Scarifier, Riverina, NSW

The Scarifier is arguably the most unusual holiday retreat in Australia. Awarded the 2015 Innovation Prize by Tourism NSW, the Scarifier is not at all scary, as the name might suggest. The name refers to its use in scarifying or scratching up the soil. No prizes for realising why this is an exciting place for a chook holiday. Each day the rather historic scarifier is towed once around a nearby paddock, while guests can follow in its multiple furrows, effortlessly snapping up the delicacies exposed without having to scratch for them.

Unsurprisingly it has become a popular venue for training young chickens, as up to 100 can easily participate at a time. The accommodation sleeps up to 200 in an imaginatively converted pigsty close by. The Scarifier has rapidly become the go-to destination for end-of-year football club holidays, and many Chicken Clubs from country areas enjoy spending weekends here, and enjoying the nearby Farm Machinery Museum.

Emlyn Williams of Milton Keynes in the UK, who notices such things, has pointed out to me that Presbyterian is an anagram of Britney Spears. We don't know whether Britney keeps chickens, however, so this may be taken as an interesting random fact of no particular relevance here.

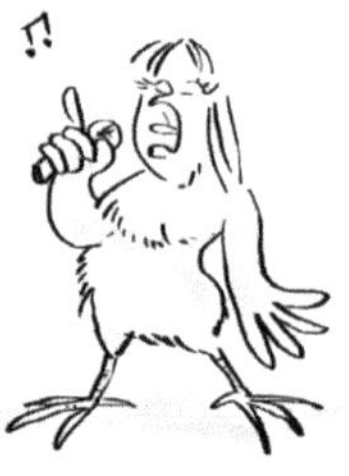

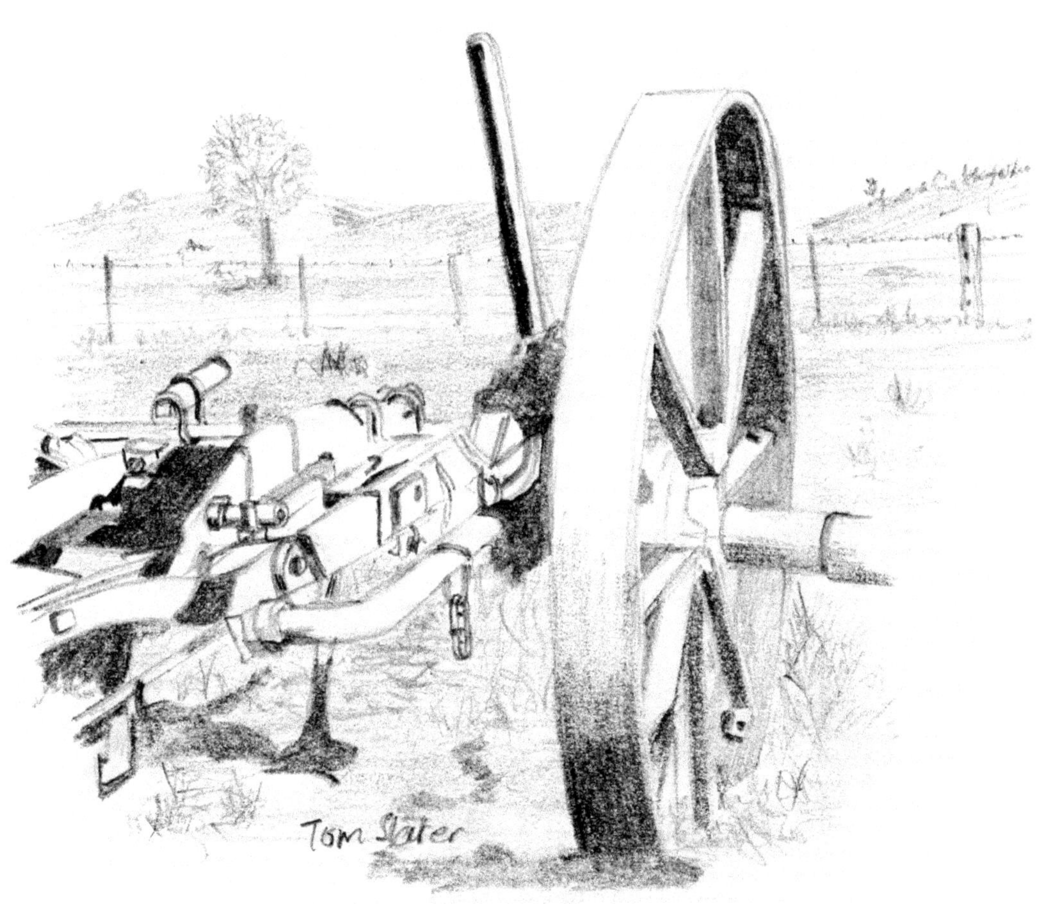
Tom Slater

Metropole, Boulder, WA

This famous old hotel was bought in 2018 by CHOOK (Chicken Hotels Of Old Kalgoorlie), and converted into a world-class conference centre for chooks.

Its famous mineshaft and tunnel, accessible directly from the main bar, provides a unique opportunity to sleep underground, while the upper rooms have been transformed into an auditorium with perches for up to 500 chickens, and breakout rooms with views across to the Super Pit, Kalgoorlie's famous open cut gold mine.

Travel to Kalgoorlie by road or the Indian Pacific train.

Feeling adventurous? You might consider joining the annual guided 'Scratch and Saunter' Chicken Safari from Perth to Kalgoorlie, which follows the 600 kms long above-ground pipeline that supplies the goldfields with water. You should allow up to six months for this, though exceptionally fit groups have done the journey in less than five.)

A visit to the Super Pit is an exciting experience for man/woman, hen/rooster, or any other living creature for that matter. Its enormity is truly mind-boggling, even given that it was opened in 1893. It would take an estimated 2.5 million chooks on top quality rations and laying no eggs an estimated 580 years to dig such a hole, which is why these days the work is done by enormous machines, without regard to the knock-on effect of major chook unemployment.

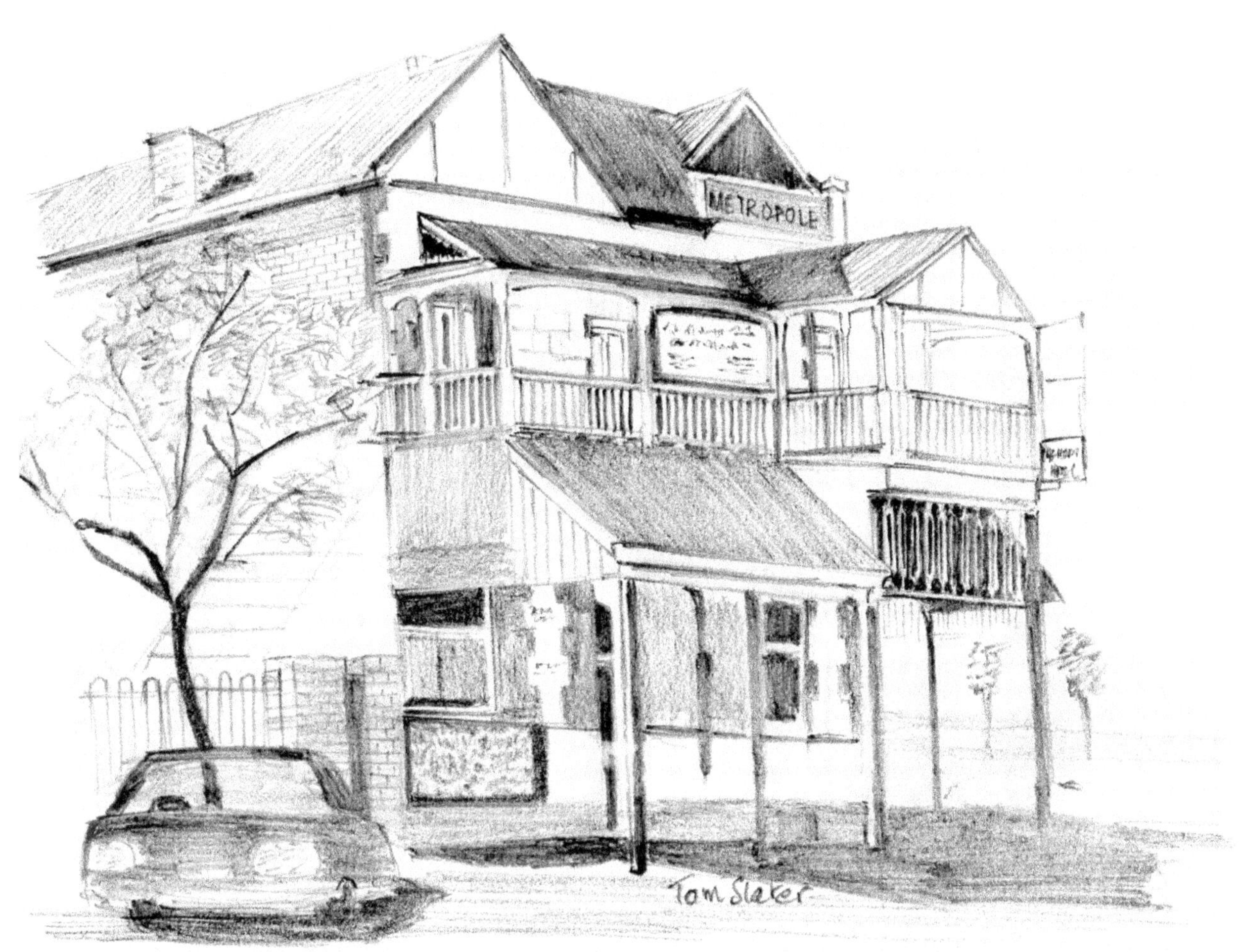
METROPOLE
Tom Slater

Shearing Shed, Yea, Vic

The wool room of this magnificent shearing shed near Yea is a combination of deluxe accommodation and adventure playground.

The historic wool press, the light and shadow cast by the skylights, and the old cane basket create an atmosphere of security and tradition.

Nooks and crannies offer a great variety of roosting options, while the management policy of leaving remnant pieces of wool around after shearing, and a practice of limited sweeping, ensures a homely chook–house ambience year-round.

This Yea property hosted the National Chook Exhibition of 1894, a first for a working sheep property in Australia.

The success of that Exhibition has ensured that this shed holds a valued place in the poultry landscape of Australia, and it has since hosted conferences for geese, turkeys and even on one occasion a national gathering of native birds. The daily tariff reflects the high standard of accommodation, but many egg farmers consider it money well spent, with their birds returning to the home coop with fresh ideas and renewed enthusiasm for laying.

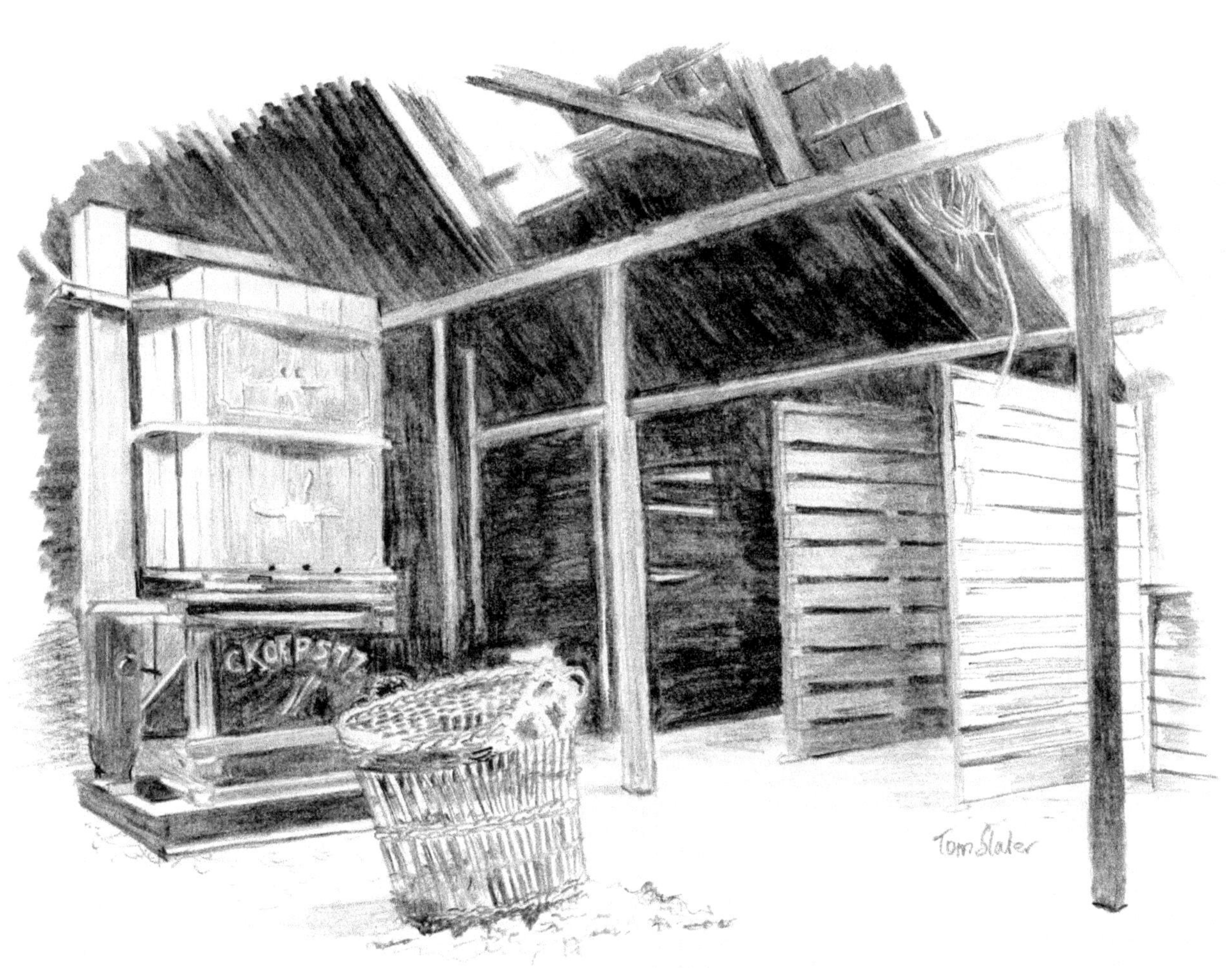
Tom Slater

Mystery Destination

This is truly a holiday for the adventurous!

The exclusive Railway Station Chotel is a package holiday, and has several unique features, the chief one being that the actual location is not revealed to guests. It is specifically designed for groups of up to 45 guests.

The hotel's own coach, which has blacked-out windows, picks up the group at a pre-arranged location suitable to the group, and guests may return home at the end of their stay without ever knowing where they have been.

Of particular interest is the massive water tank used to refill steam engines in days gone by. The old station's waiting rooms have been converted into dormitories, with perches at various heights to cater for each group's pecking order, and an old railway carriage has been turned into a theatre where groups can view old chicken movies.

As far as is known, this is the only holiday of its kind in the world, at least for chooks.

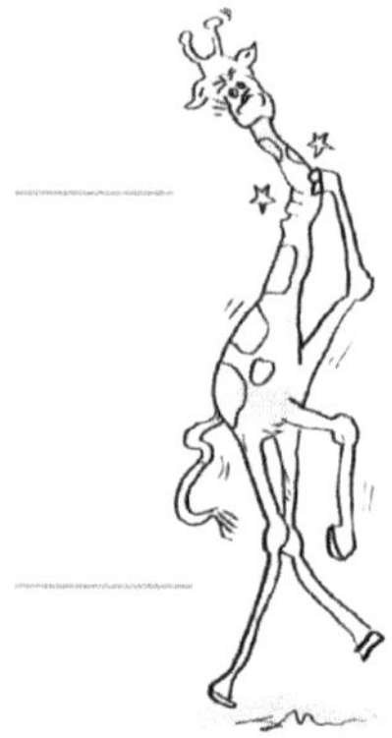

It appears that there are no 8-letter words which are an anagram of 'chicken'. If neckich was a word, that would be one.

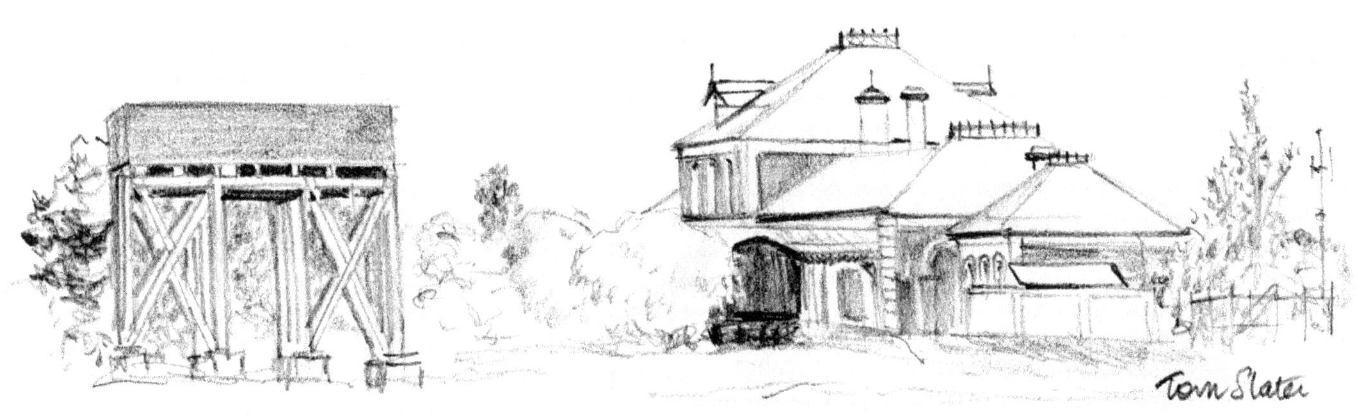
Tom Slater

Bungaree woolshed, SA

Only half a mile away from the Bungaree homestead is this large woolshed, more than 150 years old. Steeped in history and the smells of wool and sheep manure, it is especially attractive in the weeks after shearing time. Choice of bedding abounds, on a first in first served basis. Make your home in a catching pen, perch on a fence, or even in the rafters if your wings haven't been clipped. Or indulge yourself in the luxury of bedding down on a bag of daggy skirtings, or a bin of Bungaree's famous AAA Merino wool if it hasn't been baled up yet.

South Australian Egglayers holds monthly weekends here, where groups of up to 100 layers from all over the state and interstate listen to lectures on modern production techniques, as well as the history of Bungaree.

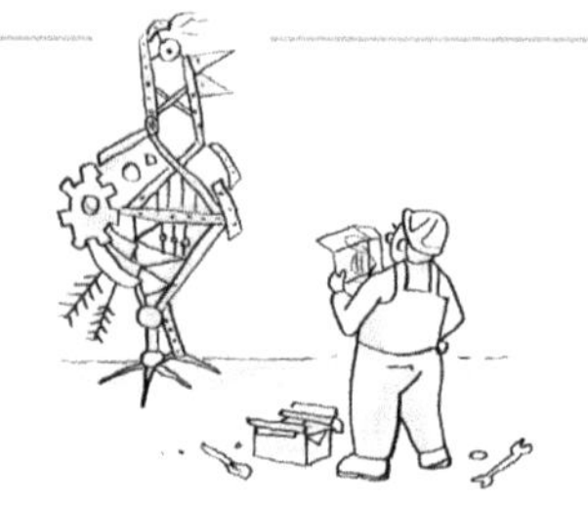

'Man has never really built a decent chicken'. Kehlog Albran, The Profit

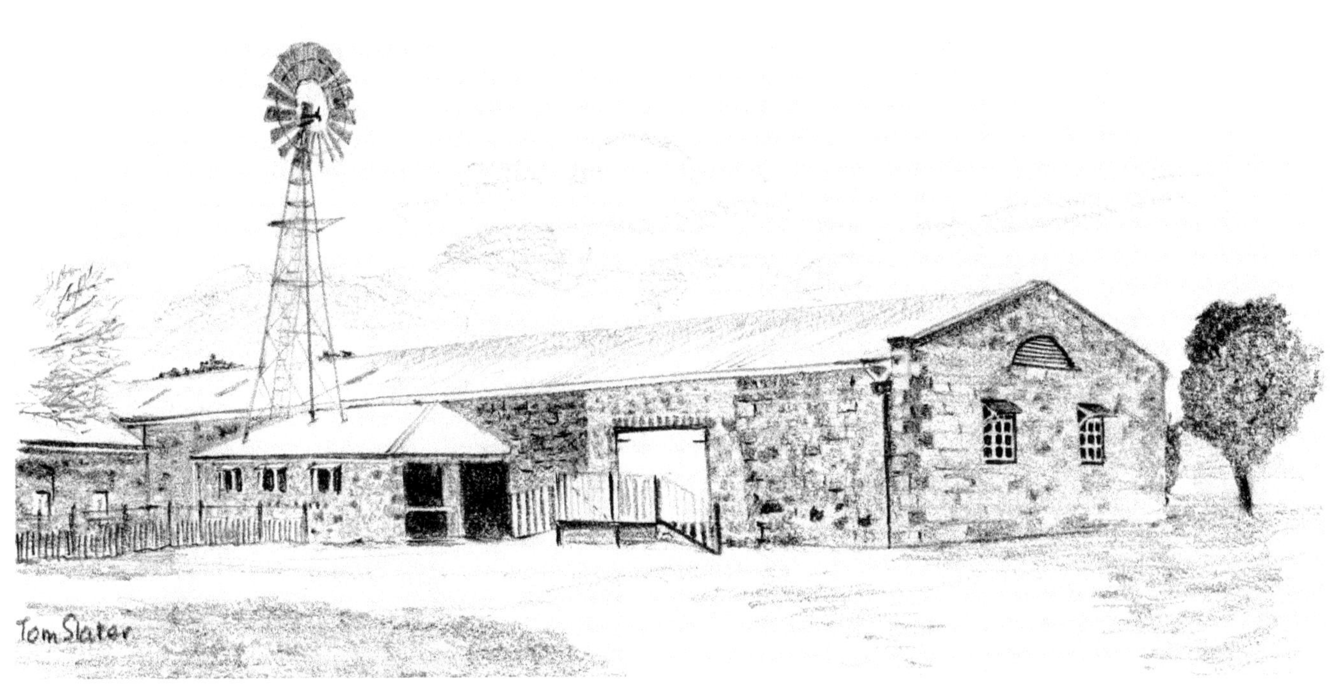
Tom Slater

Chickenland, Pleyestowe, Qld

The old Pleyestowe sugar mill, west of Mackay in Queensland, is the chicken equivalent of Disneyland.

Once it crushed nearly a million tonnes of sugar cane in a year, but it was closed in 2008. It was then purchased by Chickenland Entertainment and converted into the world's first 'Disney-type' resort exclusively for poultry.

As well as a great variety of accommodation in sheds, tanks, silos and old sugar train trucks, there is endless entertainment for which a free pass is available to live-in guests. A week is scarcely enough to try out the range of activities – the giant 'straight line' waterslide pictured, bungee jumps from the main chimney, boat rides on the adjacent Pioneer River, playing chicken with trains on the old rail lines, dodging coconuts, shooting the chutes, and much more.

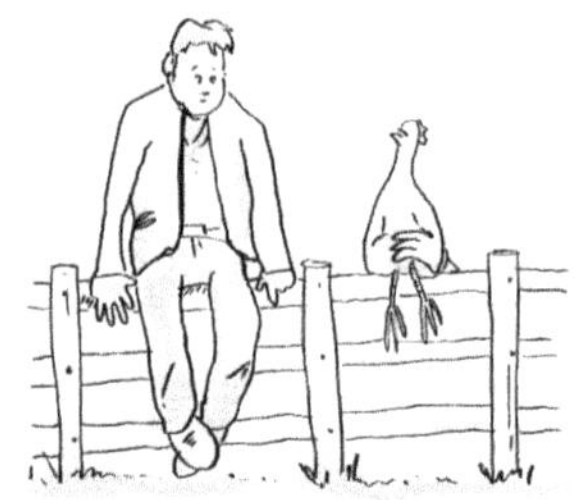

'Behaviourial resemblances' (between humans and chickens) 'do not require an exact match. One may consider them in terms of the common well-spring from which all experience flows, or in the form of a musical analogy in which the theme of sentience and its innumerable manifestations hark back to the matrix of all sentient forms.'
Karen David, founder of United Poultry Concerns on the UPC website.

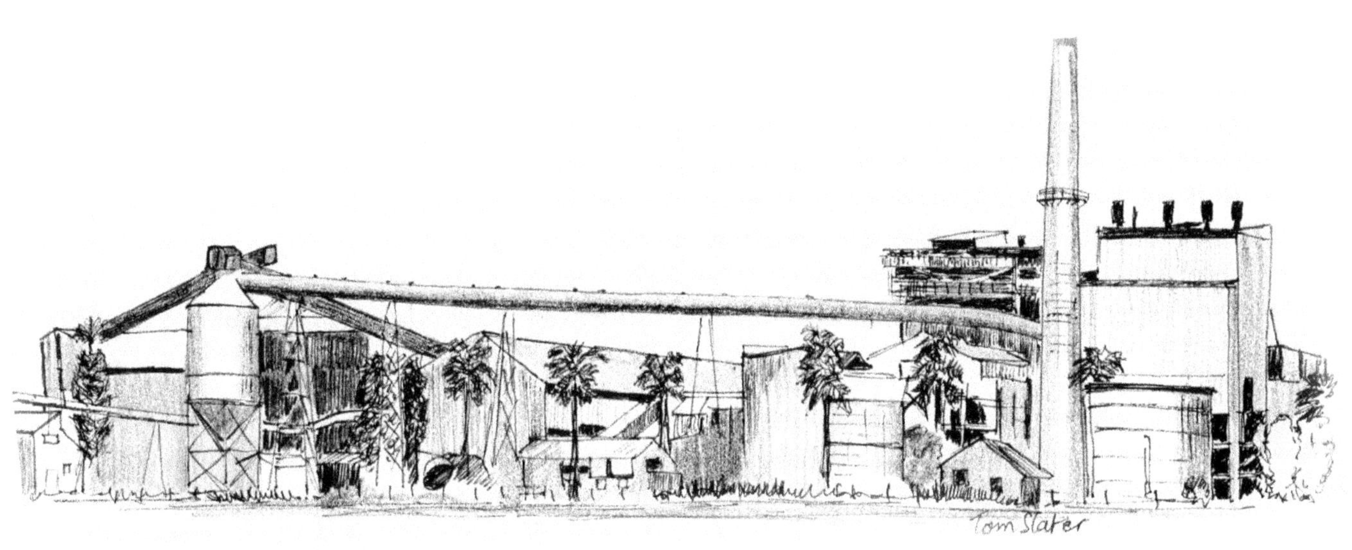
Tom Slater

Yangery Grange, Vic

At this historic farm dating back to the 19th century you are spoilt for choice. The magnificent homestead boasts a main bathroom which, according to an estate agent, 'is exceptional for today's modern use'. This odd expression seems to mean one can have a shower or a bath, or wash your hands in the hand-basin. Since none of these activities interest chooks, however, the homestead may be safely ignored.

There are multiple accommodation options, beginning with the budget accommodation in various sheds, many suitable for families. Settle in one of these sheds, and spend your days exploring the many places of interest within just a few steps or a couple of wing-flaps. There are plenty of good places to lay, if you are not having a complete break. Behind the bluestone wall the old shearing shed houses two 5-star apartments up in the loft. A dangerous old staircase is no problem for chooks, but ensures that you won't be bothered by human tourists poking around. Both units are air-conditioned.

A veritable paradise for the tourist chicken. You won't want to go home.

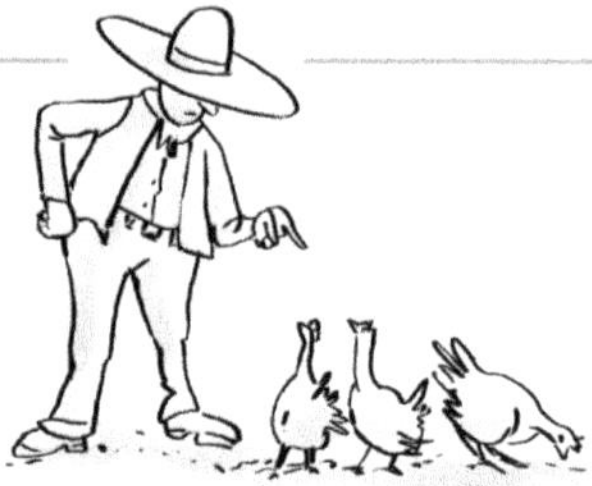

Don't count your chickens – unless you want to know how many there are.

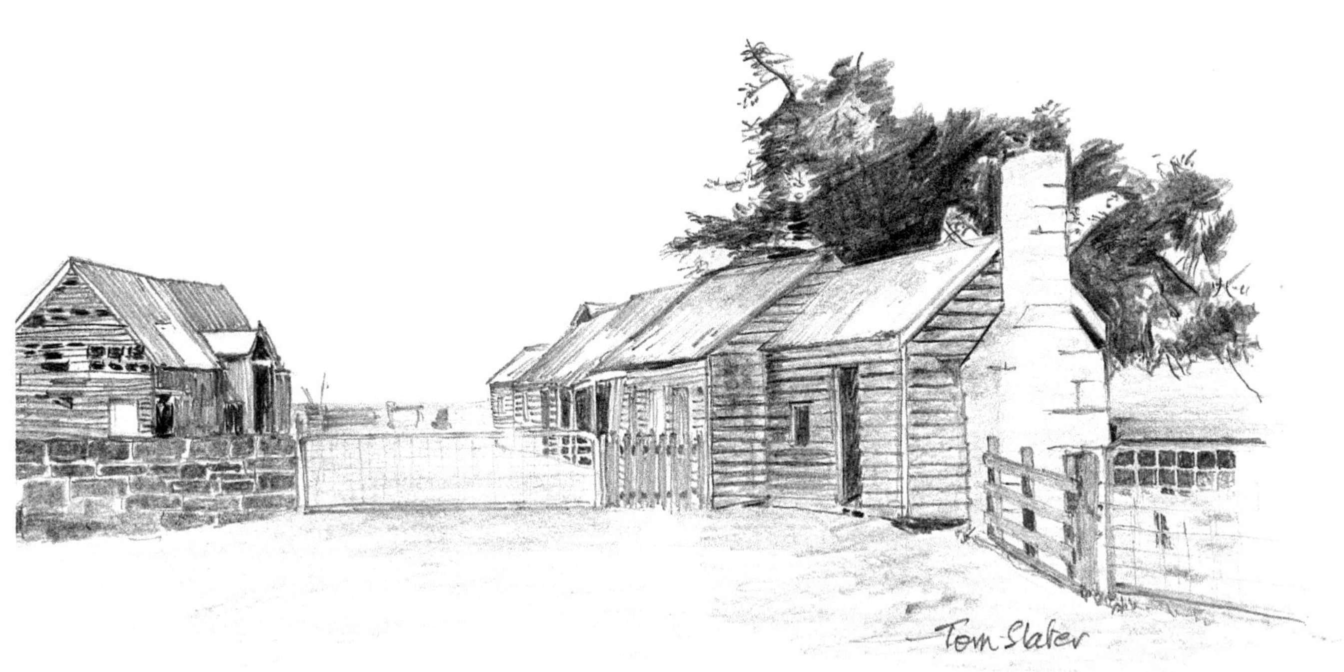
Tom Slater

ACKNOWLEDGMENTS

For his enormous contribution to this book, **Ivan Smith**, Communique Graphics. That contribution included his consummate artistic and graphic skills, including all cartoons, layout and cover design; and his generosity, patience, and intuitive understanding of what the book is about.

For their encouragement to think that it might be worth pursuing:
John Waterhouse, life-long friend and publisher of several hundred excellent Christian books under his own Albatross label; **Wapke Henson**, fun-loving and accomplished teacher of small children, and her husband **Les** – friends to laugh with through thick and thin; **Len and Jenny Creek**, farmers, long-time friends and great travelling companions; **June Slater**, my long-suffering wife who was initially (and unaccountably) sceptical about the intrinsic value of the whole exercise; and those generous people who read an early draft and offered a commendation.

For their kind permission to explore their properties:
Sally Hawker of the wonderful Bungaree Station in South Australia; and the former owner of Yangery Grange in Victoria, whose name I forget.

For everything good in our lives:
The One who made chooks and animals and trees; who gave us the graphite for pencils, the ability to build sheds, and a thousand reasons to laugh; and who enables us to love and live in peace with each other. But that's another story.

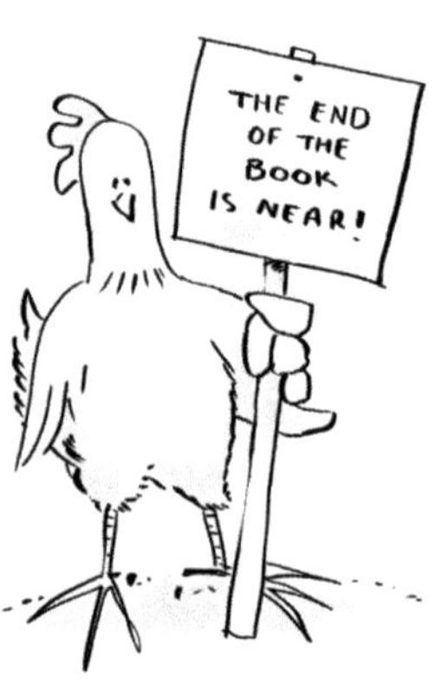
THE END OF THE BOOK IS NEAR!

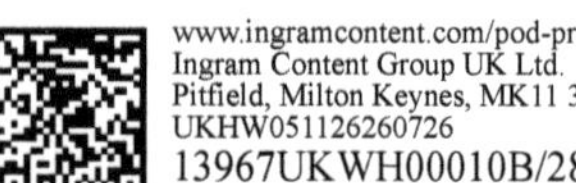

www.ingramcontent.com/pod-product-compliance
Ingram Content Group UK Ltd.
Pitfield, Milton Keynes, MK11 3LW, UK
UKHW051126260726
13967UKWH00010B/2885

9 780648 981305